MW01037421

Grace Like Rain

Experiencing the Downpour of God's Transforming Grace

Diana Kriesel

PRESS

Cover Design: Tim O'Brien – office@skystonestudios.com
Photo: Beltrami Studios

www.xulonpress.com

CONTENTS

ACKNOWLEDGEMENTS

Heartfelt appreciation to my editing team – Kevin Kriesel, Kimberly West, Nicki Shearer, and Fran Farina. I couldn't have done this without you. Thank you for reading every word (and changing several!); for countless hours of tireless focus and determination; for encouragement through the entire project; for giving up your time for mine; for bearing with me as I tried to make sense of this manuscript; and for extending your *Grace Like Rain* over my life. I pray God's favor and continued blessing over your lives.

To Tim O'Brien – for your artistic excellence in designing the outside of this book. Thanks for big grace.

To my Community Bible Church family – for your love and support throughout this journey. You are some of God's best gifts to my life.

To the team at Xulon Press – You are all amazing examples of grace! Thank you for a wonderful first publishing experience.

DEDICATIONS

Always and forever first – to my heavenly Father. Thank You for pouring Your *Grace Like Rain* over every inch of my life. Thank You for loving me back to life, and not only life, but abundant life. Every page written in this book and across my life is because of Your faithfulness and grace. I am Your daughter. You are my King.

Endless thanks to my husband Mike, who continues to rain his own soft grace on my life. Thank you for loving me and believing in me even when I couldn't believe in myself. Thank you for your incredibly amazing perspective on life, and helping me find the light in dark places. Thank you for your unwavering support through this entire project. I can't imagine doing life without you by my side. I love you.

To Kevin and Maria – my son and daughter-in-law; and Kimberly and Clint – my daughter and son-in-law. Your love for God and your dedication to His Kingdom are amazing. It has been one of my greatest privileges to watch you live for Christ, love because of Him, and raise your children for Him. Thank you for your encouragement to me through this process. Thank you for grace!

To my grandchildren – Michael, Aaron, Jesse, Jason, Lauren, Alexa, and Maia. You are my favorite world-changers. Thank you for being such pure examples of God's grace. You are His royalty, His display of glory to a world that will want to know Him just because of your lives. I love and believe in you.

To Mom and Dad – thank you for giving me life. Although you have gone home, your lives live on through mine. I look forward to an eternity with you in heaven.

In loving memory of Mary White, who has always recognized God's grace in my life, and taught me friendship grace. I learned so much about my Father through you, His daughter.

FOREWORD

Nearly 46 years ago, from behind my drum set, I looked out on the dance floor in the gymnasium of Rice Memorial High School and I saw a girl. After asking the bass player of my rock and roll band, I discovered her name was Diana. I told him, "I'm going to marry that girl." It has been 42 years since I married my high school sweetheart and we committed ourselves to one another for better or worse. In that time, I have seen God take a shy, confused, frightened young girl and turn her into a loving, confident and determined woman who also happens to be one of my favorite preachers, and it came through one of the most misunderstood phrases: *If not for the GRACE of God.*

I am so excited that Diana has used one of her many talents to share how the power of God's grace has changed her life for His glory. I could not think of a title that would better describe how it all came about than the words, *Grace Like Rain.*

You may have heard it said, "Grace is the power to change." Many people go through life wondering if that is true, as they struggle to find out just what grace is. As a pastor for over 30 years, I have met countless people who have allowed their past to get in the way of their future.

Diana is not one of those people. Through God's grace, she has discovered how the power of God's love can use life's tragedies for His glory, and how a life headed for destruction can be saved and healed by the One who died for us all.

After reading this book, you will have a better understanding of how God's grace can take even the worst situations and bring good out of them. This book is the personal journey of someone who has lived out God's grace in her life. It will help you to understand just how deep, how wide, how long, and how high God's love is for those He has created and for whom He gave His Son to die. As you read this book, I urge you to take your story, no matter how good or bad it might be, and allow God's power and love to fall on your life with *Grace Like Rain.*

– Mike Kriesel

INTRODUCTION

As I finish this book, I am a sixty-one year old daughter of God; out of which He has also blessed me to be a wife, mother, nana, sister, aunt, cousin, friend, neighbor, counselor, and pastor. I began writing this book over ten years ago. When my computer crashed, I had a rude awakening about the importance of backing up files, and the book, encased in the hard drive of my beloved laptop, went to its resting place in an electronics graveyard. Needless to say, I was discouraged at the thought of starting over from scratch. After several failed attempts to rewrite my previous work, I invited God into my process and we began to co-author my new work together. I smile as I write this because the content of these pages has almost no resemblance to what I initially had in mind. *This book is different because I am different.* I believe that God poured His grace over my earlier writing experience, to bring forth what He had in mind for this book, *Grace Like Rain.*

A funny thing happened on my mom's way to the delivery room at the hospital. Apparently I was anxious to make my entrance into this world and decided to be born in the hospital elevator, between floors. No joke. A nurse and my mom got on the elevator, and the nurse, my mom, and baby Diana got off. It would be safe to say that patience has never been my greatest virtue. My dad was spot-on in his statement about my elevator birth, when he said, "Diana's life has always been one of ups and downs." He usually followed that up with annoyance that the hospital had the nerve to add a Delivery Room charge to his bill.

Other than my inimitable elevator birth, my story may not be much different from yours; however, I share it to bring words to the often silenced pain, and hope to the heart that wonders if hope is even a possibility. This book is ultimately about putting God's grace on display so it can saturate your life as it has mine. I have experienced the downpour of a grace that brings healing and restoration to a life violated by childhood sexual abuse and raised amidst the turmoil of a home influenced by alcohol.

Although I attended church regularly, I grew up with a distorted view of God as Father. I came to believe that He was distant, aloof, and unapproachable. Add to that the shame from my victimization, and I concluded that it would be nearly impossible for me to measure up to the expectations and demands of a holy God. I always had a hunger for spiritual reality and tried to surrender my heart to religious rules and regulations. I was convinced that was what God expected. As a young adult, my heart was awakened to the beauty and the passion of the God of the Bible, and I discovered that He was not anything like what the years of religion had taught me. His grace removed the scales from my spiritual eyes, displaying a God of pure unconditional love. He revealed Himself as a personal God who desired intimacy with *me!* I am now thankful for every part of my story; the good, the bad, and the ugly; for it indeed is a story that continues to be invaded by His grace.

This brings me to the title for my book; *Grace Like Rain.* For me, grace came just like rain in so many ways, which we will visit in the pages ahead. Sometimes rain comes in a sprinkling, sometimes in a steady downpour, and other times torrentially. Sometimes it is welcomed, sometimes not. It wets the dry ground, softens hard places, leaks where we would never expect it, and at times becomes a flood. It brings deadened places to life, causes seeds to sprout, and brings lustrous growth. Even at this writing, I am watching summer rain forcefully blast its layers in sharp mischievous angles. It arrived without warning, put on quite the show, and then exited as quickly as it came. Though the rain only paid us a brief visit before it disappeared, it had great impact. Unlike a typical rainfall, it found its way into slightly opened windows and sneaked into tight places; all because of its direction. God's grace does the same thing. It shows up, gets into our tight places, and always has a purpose and direction. I love rain, and I love God's *Grace Like Rain!*

I remember my favorite encounters with rain while growing up on the shores of beautiful Lake Champlain in Vermont. When a storm was coming from the New York side of the lake, we kids would watch as the driving force of sheets of rain accelerated across the lake toward us. If we were fast enough, we would run out into the water and find a place to stand still. Then when the rain would jet closer and closer, someone would holler, "Run!" and we would try to outrun the wall of rain. No matter how fast we were, we would be overcome by the bombarding pellets of water and ultimately fall into the water laughing as the storm caught us, and then pummeled toward the beach.

We had a childlike notion that we could outrun this force of nature called rain. I love this picture because just as we cannot outrun natural rain, we cannot outrun God's *Grace Like Rain.* God's grace has a mission. That mission is you; that mission is me. It targets us, seeks us out, and never lets go of us. It is forgiving, forgetting, restoring, transforming, and consuming. It levels the playing field so we can see that God had every one of us in mind when He chose to pour His ever-flowing grace out on humanity through the sacrifice of His Son, Jesus Christ. When God's grace finds us, we are captured by His unconditional love. When we allow His grace to invade our belief system, He floods it with the truth of His Word to heal and restore us. God's *Grace Like Rain* is beyond amazing.

There are so many pockets of residual emotional pain from our history that can impede our spiritual growth. As we identify them and apply God's Word to them, we make great strides toward becoming restored, liberated, and functioning for His Kingdom. Woven through these chapters are glimpses into my little girl heart, sharing how God rained His amazing grace on every shattered part of my life, restoring me to wholeness in Him. He took me from a place of insecurity, confusion, shame, fear, and feeling like I didn't belong; to a place of fulfillment, peace, joy and ultimately a place of belonging in Him. As a result of God's *Grace Like Rain*, I have not only made peace with my past, but I have experienced the power of His trans-forming love.

I have thought and prayed about how much I should reveal in sharing my story in this book. Many authors give intimate details of abuse, names of characters, and lengthy descriptions of trauma. You will discover that I intentionally omit names and details concerning family troubles and the sexual abuse that I endured. I am not eager to share the pain, or those responsible; for God's grace has enabled me to move forward. I value and respect each person's right to share their own story should they decide to do so. Since God has graced-over my life in ways I could have never imagined, I have chosen to limit my story to my own personal experience.

A trusted college professor who had become acquainted with my story through various assignments told me, "Diana, your story is long overdue." One of my difficulties in writing was in considering how much I wanted to step into the pages with my own experience, and how often I should use my story as a teaching. I think it has come to be both. I am a fairly private person, and *Grace Like Rain* contains some very intimate elements. My desire in sharing my story was not to share what I *wanted* it to be, nor what I thought it *should* be, but what it *was*.

My favorite part of sharing my journey is when I get to switch gears from the pain, and what went so wrong, to my healing and what God did to make things so right. I love to tell how my **history** becomes **His story**, and how His *Grace Like Rain* poured over my life and restored me to wholeness. That is why I have chosen to make brief visits to the sadness and trauma so we can move into the process, discovery, healing, and ultimately, my transformation.

God's grace has taken me from a place of fear and insecurity to confidence in Him as my heavenly Father, and a freedom I never dared to imagine. Each day I find myself being awakened to the possibilities, adventures, and surprises that He has for me. I hope that as you travel through these pages, you will discover new truths about God's grace for your own life, and invite others to experience His *Grace Like Rain* for their lives.

God has used His written Word in so many ways as He has saturated my heart with His grace. Psalm 107:20 says, *"He sent His word and healed them"* (NASB). For this reason, I have shared verses that have ministered to me along my journey toward restoration. At the end of each chapter, I have set apart a section called: ***Grace Like Rain from His Word***, listing Scriptures God has used in my life.

I pray that these verses will bring hope, encouragement, peace, and healing. No doubt He will add to this inventory as you allow His grace-filled Word to saturate your heart.

It is now in your hands: a book about my story with God's *Grace Like Rain* splashed all over it. You will discover that though the scenes are not always pleasant, they are real. Though my pain and brokenness came primarily as a result of childhood sexual abuse, I believe the journey toward hope and healing can be applied to any heart that longs for wholeness. I realize there are countless sources of emotional wounds, and just as many books written with guidelines for healing.

I invite you into your own walk toward change: facing the truth about past and present experiences; discovering the love and grace of our heavenly Father; learning to take down protective barriers that ultimately keep us from our own recovery; embracing the liberating power of forgiveness, and discovering that God has a purpose for your life.

My hope is that each of us comes to a greater understanding of the unconditional, transforming love of God and that we experience His amazing grace as it rains redemptive healing over our pain, fear, anger, and loss. I look forward to sharing how God has brought me lasting peace and joy. Is there life after abuse? Absolutely! And not just life; *abundant life!*

I am humbled that you chose to take the time to enter into my story. So many of you have encouraged and supported me along the way with prayer and words of affirmation, providing the impetus to keep on going. Thank you for being yet another of God's great examples to me of *Grace Like Rain.*

– Diana Kriesel

chapter one

GIVE GRACE A CHANCE

"See to it that no one misses the grace of God."
Hebrews 12:15

*"For it is by grace you have been saved, through faith
— and this not from yourselves, it is the gift of God."*
Ephesians 2:8

Bookstore shelves are filled with books on grace. We say grace before meals, we name baby girls Grace. iPods are loaded with playlists of songs proclaiming God's grace. Most of us grew up singing *Amazing Grace*. The Bible has so many things to say about grace. It speaks of a *spirit of grace. Great grace. Abundant grace. Sufficient grace. Saving grace. Enabling grace. Reigning grace. Surpassing grace. Glorious grace. Increasing grace. Grace and peace. Grace and truth. Grace and power. Evidence of grace. The provision of grace. Being under grace. Being full of grace. Being chosen by grace. Being anointed with grace. Wearing a garland of grace. Excelling in grace. The gift of grace.* Quite a resumé, isn't it? Pretty much wherever, however, whenever; grace can show up in a myriad of ways.

What is grace?

Many of us learned an acronym for grace: **G**od's **R**iches **A**t **C**hrist's **E**xpense, which is often used to describe grace. I do better appreciating and experiencing grace than I do defining it. Every time I think I understand God's grace, He uses it to turn something upside-down or inside-out, and I stand in awe once again. Grace grabs us, shakes the life back into us and sets our feet on solid ground. Grace finds what we try to hide in darkness and welcomes it into the light; all while loving us and dispelling our fears. Grace moves in when life moves out, and chases us down when we stray off course. When God's grace splashes into one area of our life, it isn't restricted to our expectations, but flings itself wherever needed. It's a life-force doing what it does best: conforming us into the image of Jesus Christ. It targets an area that has been wrecked by life and does what only grace can do: restores, heals, and forgives; all to bring us back to God's original intent.

I wish there was a whole chapter in the Bible telling us what grace is, like First Corinthians 13 describes love, but there isn't. Instead, God puts grace on display in and through His Son, and demonstrates the work of grace through the lives of people throughout Scripture. We will visit a few of those Old and New Testament friends to help develop our own personal understanding of grace. The more I experience His great grace, the more I fall in love with the Giver of grace.

God's grace overpowers us, enables us, forgives us, is a result of His love, and is something we don't deserve. God's grace is so incredible; words are elusive in describing it. Grace is all about Jesus. It's about Him, because of Him, from Him, and through Him. Too often, we limit our understanding of grace by assuming that it has only one purpose – our salvation. If the only work of grace would have been to save each of us from the hell we ultimately deserved, I would be eternally grateful. But it is so much greater, deeper, richer, and stronger. Grace is not cheap; in fact it is a gift from God that came at an indescribable price. Let's take grace out of its box. Let's allow God to expose every part of our lives to His amazing, transforming gift called grace.

The grace of God is not passive, by any means. It is an active, living force in the life of every child of God. Grace draws us toward increased intimacy with the Father and decreased dependency on our self-will; while releasing a divine enablement to walk in our God-ordained destiny. Once we have experienced its freeing movement in us, we will then be consumed with a contagious desire to extend it toward others – making us true grace-carriers.

No matter what you have been through, God's grace is ready and waiting; eager to saturate you with His love. Grace is Jesus personified, Holy Spirit delivered. Grace can rework our perceptions of the past, renew our hearts in the present, and shape our responses in the future. Grace is God's explosive entrance into our life, carrying His purpose and plans for our destiny; in spite of our mess, and because of our mess. He is Redeemer of not only our eternal soul, but our existing stuff. I am crazy about God's grace!

My hope is that this book will inspire you to give God's grace a chance in your life. I encourage you to allow His *Grace Like Rain* to saturate every area of your heart, mind, and memory; so that you become a display of His glory. This is a win-win for us. He applies grace to our devastated places and transforms them into something amazing so we can proclaim: *"The Lord is our strength and song"* (Exodus 15:2). When His grace gets its grip on us, we will never want to live any other way. Actually, grace has always had a grip on us; we just haven't had a grip on grace, perhaps because we didn't recognize it. When we do, we will experience His soft strength in our lives, and it will give rise to a new song in our hearts. He wants to birth an awareness of His grace in our lives; a living, transforming grace that can't be contained.

I will share brief overviews of experiences of my painful places and then transition to how God entered with His *Grace Like Rain.* If my personal hurts had not collided with grace, I cannot imagine where I would be today. I want to take you past my drama and into my grace journey. I hope to present you with a picture of the brokenness of a girl whose heart needed a flood of God's grace, and how that grace showed up. My prayer is that your own gallery of grace will expand and explode with fresh personal revelation of His love for you.

No one likes physical pain; we avoid it whenever we can. Given a choice between a pill and an injection, we would likely opt for the pill. Similarly, when it comes to life experiences, we prefer pleasure over pain. Life happens. Hurts come. Wounds are inflicted. Losses occur. What we experience as children contributes to the way we look at ourselves. When we are abused, we conclude that we are broken, different, or defective. So many adults just want to push the delete button on painful childhood memories and move on. This doesn't work for a few reasons. First, it's impossible to actually remove what we experienced. Second, when placed under the restorative grace and power of God, our pain and sorrow can be transformed into evidence of the healing power of God.

After over thirty years of leading support groups and counseling women and girls who have been victimized by childhood sexual abuse, I have discovered that those who choose to give God access to their pain are positioned to gain profound wisdom, compassion, insight and strength. Something incredible happens in our process of transformation when we give grace a chance. That's what I am submitting to you today. *Give God's grace a chance.* You have nothing to lose and everything to gain. Deep within the heart of every woman I counseled was a private hope and longing for peace, love, and truth. That longing isn't self-instilled. It is put there by God.

When we were created, God knew what we would go through. He has put within our spiritual DNA the resilience to not only survive, but thrive, so we can take our place in His plan for us. *"For I know the plans I have for you," declares the Lord, "plans to prosper you and not to harm you, plans to give you hope and a future"* (Jeremiah 29:11). He knows what He has in store for us, and wants to introduce us to our destiny. It's important that we learn to trust God enough to let His grace soften our hearts, and take down our walls of protection. When the walls come down, we can begin to move forward.

When we give God's grace a chance, we discover that He does not see us as broken, damaged, or irreversibly crippled. He sees us as His loved and valued children. I desperately needed to know this truth, because it gave me the courage to release my pain and hurt to Him. When we release our wounds to the Lord, He gives us *"beauty instead of ashes, the oil of gladness instead of mourning, and a garment of praise instead of a spirit of despair"* (Isaiah 61:3a NKJV).

I have learned that when we open the door of our broken, wounded heart to God, He graciously enters and transforms us into the image of His Son, Jesus. Our heavenly Father takes a heart that has been crushed by pain and saturates it with His healing love and grace. He not only heals us, but He uses our transformation to show off

His work through our lives: *"They will be called oaks of righteousness, a planting of the Lord for the display of His splendor"* (v. 3b). Our upside-down-ness turned aright, becomes a display of His splendor. In short, He takes our *mess* and makes it His *message* to others.

I understand that it may seem a bit dreamy to imagine that a childhood riddled with pain can be transformed into something beautiful, but it can; when we give God's grace a chance. If God desires your restoration more than you do, then why not allow His desire to override yours? Consistently in Scripture we see broken, wounded men and women of God attach their wagon to God's dream for them, and He always comes through. I have come to learn that my life is not a mystery to be solved but a treasure to be discovered, and so is yours. Just as the pain we endured as children was real, so is the God-planted resilience that resides deep within us.

God desires that our childhood pain would birth a spiritual search in our hearts, leading us straight to Him. We are plagued with questions such as, *Why me? Where do I belong? How will I ever find joy and peace? Where was God in all of my pain; and where is He now?* I will admit that as a little girl I couldn't have verbalized those questions, but they were there. At the time, I was more consumed with self-protection, isolation, confusion about trust, and ultimately survival. It wasn't until I was a teenager that I got a glimmer of hope that there must be life after abuse.

As I share with you the various nuggets of truth I found along my journey, I hope you will also give grace a chance. Honestly, what do you have to lose? In Galatians 2:21, the Apostle Paul says, *"I do not set aside the grace of God."* If grace is God's free gift to us to enable our healing and restoration, why would we set it aside? When we set the grace of God aside, we frustrate that grace and imply that it was not necessary for Jesus to die because we thought we could somehow fix ourselves.

Most women, when they finally arrived at my office, were motivated to come out of a desire to be healed and restored. They wanted to discover God's purpose for their lives as they embraced the possibility of permanently breaking free from the chains of their abuse. It is important to understand how the pain from the past is affecting our lives today. Grace allows us to see our wounds without picking our scabs, look at our lives without beating up on ourselves, and recognize our weaknesses without getting stuck there. Ignoring our wounds is just as bad as picking our scabs. If we ignore an open, gaping wound, it will become infected. Ignored or picked, neither heals.

When a person endures a painful childhood, she cultivates a keen awareness and vigilance as a method of survival. Her pain sharpens her ability to listen attentively and keep an eye on what's happening around her. This is initially developed in self-protection; however, God rains grace on this sensitivity, and uses it for our good as we move toward restoration. He redeems our sensitivity, teaching us to be sensitive to His Spirit and sensitive to others.

When we have learned to protect our heart, sometimes it's difficult to let our guard down. No matter what you have been through, will you consider letting your guard down for One; the Creator of the universe, your Creator? He wants to accompany you on this journey into the deepest place of your pain. He is safe. He has one intention: to love you to life. He has your best interest in mind and wants to set you completely free. If you try to attain healing from your past without Him, you will end up frustrated and confused.

Once you have asked Jesus to forgive your sins, and become Lord of your life, you will discover that He is safe, and it is not a risk for you to allow Him to heal and restore you. Let Him be God, and you be you. He will not only apply grace to your places of pain, but He will also supply grace for your journey. As He pours His *Grace Like Rain* over you, He will use your life to draw others to the same hope you have discovered in Him.

Give grace a chance to reawaken your inborn desire to discover who God says you are. Be patient with yourself on your journey toward healing and restoration. Scars from childhood may remain, but rather than sting with memories of pain, your scars can become God's trophies of your victory. Daniel 11:33 declares: *"The people who know their God shall be strong, and carry out great exploits"* (NKJV). As you come to know God on an even more intimate level, you will find new strength in Him, and together you will accomplish great things. His grace offers what faith reaches for. Where we used to timidly approach God with tiny thimbles hoping He would fill them, we can learn to run with abandoned hearts and bottomless buckets of expectation that not only will He fill us, but He will flood us with His love, grace, healing, and hope.

The apostle Paul was intimate with God's grace. If anyone understood the grace of God, it was Paul. He started out as the chief of sinners, and transitioned to be the chief of the apostles. How? One word: grace. When up against seemingly insurmountable circumstances, he would face off with God, and ultimately face off with grace. He didn't learn grace in a book; he learned it from experience. The Lord told him, *"My grace is sufficient for you, for My power is made perfect in weakness"* (2 Corinthians 12:9). Grace loves to land on our weakness to show off God's strength. When we bump into those brick walls of life with no place to turn, that's exactly where we meet up with grace. Paul wrote in Colossians 1:27, *"Christ in you, the hope of glory."* Christ is the embodiment of grace. As a son or daughter of God, Christ is in you. Connect the dots: Grace in Christ. Christ in you. Grace in you!

It was grace that caused Jesus to tell us, *"You did not choose Me, but I chose you"* (John 15:16 NKJV). Paul knew he was chosen by God. He knew that God had great plans for him. He reveled in the grace of God that forgave him for what he had done as it ushered him into his destiny. How does one go from being a murderer, to being the greatest of the apostles? Living in grace, and living out of grace. Paul knew the strength of grace and walked in it.

Each one of us can know God's grace and redemption through Christ, and find purpose to live the abundant life He has promised for us. As children of our Creator God, we are brimming over with creativity, but we get distracted, distressed and dismayed by our painful issues. Grace can revive an imagination that has slipped into a coma. He designed us with a capacity for ongoing discovery and revelation of who He is, who we are, and what He's up to in this world.

Grace Like Rain from His Word:

"I ask the God of our Master, Jesus Christ, the God of glory — to make you intelligent and discerning in knowing Him personally, your eyes focused and clear, so that you can see exactly what it is He is calling you to do, grasp the immensity of this glorious way of life He has for Christians, oh, the utter extravagance of His work in us who trust Him — endless energy, boundless strength!" (Ephesians 1:18-19 MSG).

"Having been justified by His grace, we might become heirs having the hope of eternal life" (Titus 3:7).

"In Him we have redemption through His blood, the forgiveness of sins, in accordance with the riches of God's grace that He lavished on us with all wisdom and understanding" (Ephesians 1:7-8).

"My grace is sufficient for you, for My power is made perfect in weakness" (2 Corinthians 12:9).

chapter two

THERE WAS NO CHAIR FOR ME

I know. An odd title, right? But it's the best place to start, the best window-in so you can see the shape I was in and how great my need was for God and His *Grace Like Rain* to pour over my life. Most of us can remember playing *Musical Chairs* as children. It's a game with any number of participants and one less chair than the number of players. The chairs are arranged in a circle facing outward with the children standing just outside the chairs. As the music begins, the children walk in unison around the circle of chairs. At random times, the music is suddenly stopped and all the players rush to sit in chairs. The player who is left without a chair is eliminated from the game and one chair is removed to ensure that there will always be one less chair than there are children. The music resumes and the cycle is repeated until there are two children remaining, but only one chair. When the music stops one last time, the child who can land in the chair is considered the winner, while the other is left standing.

This game called *Musical Chairs* is a good illustration of my heart as a little girl. Through the intent of no one,

I somehow came to feel that life around me was always "one chair short" – so that whenever I tried to find my place, I could find none. All the seats seemed to be taken. When we grow up in a dysfunctional family (and who doesn't?), we find ourselves unintentional participants in the games played; games constructed to keep the family system moving. In the game I found myself in called *Musical Chairs*, the children marched to the hypnotizing beat made by scotch bottles, beer cans, confusion, and private pain. It is a tune that commands cooperation, and somehow each family member fades in and marches in step, around and around.

As the music plays its predictable melody, each one marches perfectly, being careful to comply with the music makers. Then, without warning, the music stops and worried children scurry to find their chair, only to find that there is always one short. I was marching to music that seemed to take me nowhere, and I grew up feeling like there was no chair for me when the music stopped. I felt alone even though surrounded; ashamed and confused, standing in a room that didn't make any sense to me.

Let me back up a bit. I was the fourth of ten children born into our family. When my mother was pregnant with me, both of my brothers contracted spinal meningitis, and the older one, just a toddler, died. Needless to say, my mom hoped with all of her heart that the baby she carried in her womb would be a boy. After all, she had just lost a son, who could blame her? Then came me. Not blue, but pink. Not Ken, but Barbie. Over the years growing up, it became clear to me that I was the girl that should have been the boy my mom had hoped for. To my young mind that equaled major disappointment. My logic concluded that I was one big mistake.

I dealt with this by trying to be the good girl, the good daughter. I developed a performance-based mentality and lived my life to please my mom, yet felt I never could. At the same time, I was desperately trying to win my daddy's heart by fishing, hunting, and helping in his tool room. Boy junk. I loved it whenever I could come along-side my dad, and I was willing to do whatever was needed to play the role of the boy. Bait the hook. Carry the tools. Dig the holes. Put up the fence. Clean the fish. Freeze in the duck blind. I did just about anything in an effort to make up for not being a boy to my mom; while being a tomboy to win my dad. I somehow lost *me* in the process.

Those of us who grew up in troubled families most likely can identify with this feeling of not belonging, even in our own homes. We learned to anticipate what our parents expected in advance, so we could try to do what pleased them. We learned to numb our feelings to lessen our own sense of undesirability. Even though we may have been told that we had a place of belonging, we most likely had to guess what that meant. I never felt like I had found my niche, my place in the family system.

I cluttered my life with various strategies for belonging; thinking that if I could just figure out what to do to be accepted, maybe I would feel like I belonged. Trying to earn a sense of belonging is like trying to pick up Jell-o with a toothpick. As hard as I would try, sooner or later my efforts would fail, leaving me once again feeling like I didn't fit.

Between the ages of eight and eleven, I was sexually abused by the chief of police in a small Vermont town. Although he was a friend of our family, I was terrified of him. At random times, my mom would drive me to his house for *visits*. The closer we got, I could feel the knot in my stomach get tighter. The chief would take me into the back room, where I would listen in fearful obedience as he spelled out the rules. If I did as I was told I wouldn't have to face the looming "or else." I was not to cry or yell, and *never, ever* was I to tell anyone what happened.

As soon as he would begin to remove my clothes and touch my skin with his rough hands, I would feel cold and my body would begin to shiver. I would feel myself stiffen, and then I would go numb. I would bite my lip to keep myself from screaming. When that didn't work I would hold my breath or shut my eyes tight until it was over. I hated that he would rub himself against me, and I felt like throwing up every time he made me touch him. I wished I could crawl inside myself and disappear. I learned to shut down. I would be still, detached, silent. Each time it happened, I got more skilled at shutting down and going somewhere else in my mind until it ended . . . until the next time.

Though we were behind closed doors, I kept thinking my mom couldn't be far, and that was confusing. I would get lost in the fantasy that she would miss me, look for me, and then barge into the room to rescue me, but it never happened. After we returned home each time, I would run to the bathroom and curl up in the corner of the bathtub, making sure the running water was loud enough to muffle my sobs. Tears traced winding paths down my cheeks and lost themselves in the bath water below. The nights after visits to the chief were the worst. Alone in the dark and unable to sleep, my mind would rewind the events of the day. I couldn't stop the pictures. Fear found a stronghold in the dark silence. It would fuel my sense of isolation and shame, and at the same time it would breed powerlessness and insecurity. I hated nighttime.

I was confused, to say the least. How does a little girl make sense of being a girl, but feeling a girl wasn't wanted; having a friend of the family violate her and yet her whole world seems oblivious to it; wanting to belong but having no clue where to sit down and know her place? I vacillated between wanting to work hard to find my place, and hiding out so I could be invisible. These choices produced internal chaos and made me wonder if I wanted to belong at all. Abuse is a teacher that takes us to a bridge where there are no answers, only questions. How does a little girl make sense of a world where questions remain unanswered? She doesn't.

I share this snapshot of my history to invite you into the journey of my heart. Sometimes in order to go forward, we must look back to visit the stage on which our struggle for belonging took place. I went from feeling as if *there was no chair for me, to* eventually encountering the love of my heavenly Daddy, who has continued to pour His *Grace Like Rain over* every broken part, bringing restoration to my life. If I had not had an encounter with God's grace, I would have remained trapped in an abyss of misery. His love is never ending, and His grace is ever flowing. I am thankful for a God who intercepted *the game* and healed my heart. Now the music He plays never stops because He is the joy of my life.

Grace Like Rain from His Word:

"And you He made alive, who were dead in trespasses and sins, in which you once walked according to the course of this world, according to the prince of the power of the air, the spirit who now works in the sons of disobedience, among whom also we all once conducted ourselves in the lusts of our flesh, fulfilling the desires of the flesh and of the mind, and were by nature children of wrath, just as the others. But God, who is rich in mercy, because of His great love with which He loved us, even when we were dead in trespasses, made us alive together with Christ (by grace

you have been saved), and raised us up together, and made us sit together in the heavenly places in Christ Jesus, that in the ages to come He might show the exceeding riches of His grace in His kindness toward us in Christ Jesus. For by grace you have been saved through faith, and that not of yourselves; it is the gift of God, not of works, lest anyone should boast. For we are His workmanship, created in Christ Jesus for good works, which God prepared beforehand that we should walk in them" (Ephesians 2:1-10 NKJV).

Whereas the game called *Musical Chairs* left me with no sense of belonging or security, God used the healing power of His Word to help me walk away from the pain of the past. I realized I no longer needed to seek out a place to belong in the chaos of my yesterdays. As a result of Christ's love, I can live present to the moment, and I have found my place of acceptance in Him. I march to new music, a rhapsody written in heaven, a song that never ends.

Belonging has little to do with our physical world and everything to do with our relationship with God. Belonging begins in that deep place within our spirit where God makes His home in us. Jesus made a way for us to truly belong. God used the verses in the second chapter of Ephesians to give me His perspective on my place of belonging. It declares that though we have walked to the beat of evil done against us, no matter what we have endured, two little words changed everything for us: *But God!* It says, *"But God, who is rich in mercy, because of His great love with which He loved us, even when we were dead in trespasses, made us alive together with Christ (by grace you have been saved), and raised us up together, and made us sit together in the heavenly places in Christ Jesus."*

Abuse happens. *But God.* Our heart is broken. *But God.* People abandon us. *But God.* Each of us could make a list of ways we were hurt. He fills in the rest with *But God.*

He made provision for us. As a result of His great love for us, He took us from our deadened place in sin, made us alive together with Jesus, and then raised us up and **seated** us with Christ! **Seated!** A chair for me! A chair for you! No longer can life keep us from belonging once we become a child of God. We belong because we are His. We matter. We have value. This one truth has blasted through my ungodly belief system and shifted everything. It is a foundational truth for each of us to replace any lie that we have come to believe with the truth of the power of His great love for us.

God created each of us to be significant human beings on this earth: sons and daughters who know their place and know they belong. We try to convince ourselves that it doesn't really matter, but it does. It's supposed to matter. God wants us to know that if something matters to us, it matters to Him. When we admit and identify our need to know our place, we can move toward healing the hurt and discovering who we are and that we matter. You matter to God, and though you may not realize it yet, you matter to others. Let Him take you from that place of finding *no chair* to the amazing truth that He thought so much of you that He made a place for you next to His Son, Jesus. It's true. *If you are a child of God, you are seated with Christ right now.*

God has walked me through many classrooms which He has used to retrain my brain to know the truth about myself, and the truth about Him. His classrooms are the best because if we miss a lesson, skip a class, or neglect our homework, He already has another lesson plan. My training ground may be different from yours, but His goal is the same for all of us: to teach us to walk in His Truth and His purpose for our lives, and for His glory.

chapter three

THE DAY I LOST MY VOICE

I was nine years old when I finally got the courage to tell my mom about the chief's abuse. I can't tell you why it took me a year. Maybe it was the heart of a little girl who secretly hoped it would all stop. All I know is that something in me went increasingly numb each time he touched me, each time he made me touch him, each time he tried to convince me that I was special. It didn't take me long to realize that special really meant set apart for his pleasure. Not really special at all.

I remember the long rides to his house where the abuse occurred. I would stare out the window and watch everything turn blurry the closer we got to his house. I would feel myself go numb; the kind of numbness you experience when your arm falls asleep to the point that you can't feel it or move it. There seems to be a sudden disconnect from a part of you that once moved effortlessly, but now renders you powerless.

By the time we would arrive at the chief's house, I would almost be robotic. One foot in front of the other, up the front steps, through the door to hell. The ride home was pretty much the same, only in reverse. I would thaw out the further we got from his house and as my own street came into focus, I would switch gears, preparing myself to once again function as the big sister, the good helper, the girl-that-should've-been-a-boy. I wondered how long it would continue. I wondered how long I could take it. I knew the touching had to stop.

Finally, one day after we got back from the chief's house, in desperation I thought, *If I could just tell my mom, surely she would save me from this monster.* I even felt guilty about thinking of him as a monster because it was in such conflict with how my parents spoke of him: wonderful, kind, giving, caring, generous. Seriously? But maybe, just maybe, if I did tell her, she would believe me and make it stop. My parents had always drilled into us the importance of telling the truth. I had to tell someone. *This can't keep happening to me.* I needed someone to intervene and rescue me. My mind raced across the terrain of possibilities. *If I tell, maybe he will go to jail, and he won't be able to hurt anyone else. Wait, do chiefs of police actually go to jail?* If I didn't tell it would continue. Tell. Not tell. Back and forth I went. Finally, I decided I was going to tell.

I waited and watched for the moment to finally tell my mom. One afternoon I followed her around until she noticed me. "Diana, what do you want?" It was more of an annoying remark than a question. I couldn't discern whether my stomach felt sick at the thought of telling my mom, or the dread of more abuse by the chief. If I told, my unbearable shame and filth would be exposed. I decided to go for it and blurted out, "It's about the chief. I have to tell you something about the chief." She reeled around and said, "What?" I said, "Uh, he does stuff to me. Really bad stuff." I felt my eyes burning as they filled with tears, but I steeled myself so they wouldn't pour down my cheeks; at least not now, not in front of my mother. With a blank stare, she asked, "What are you talking about?"

I didn't think she would become my best friend and hold me close to her, patting my back and telling me it would never happen again. But I was shaken by her anger toward me. Now I was sorry that I even brought it up. I was terrified. My voice became more timid as hers grew increasingly angry. "When you bring me to his house, he takes me to the back room and touches me." There. I got it out. I lowered my head in shame. My face was hot with embarrassment. *What if she asks for details? I could* **never** *tell her exactly what he did. Maybe now that it was out I would be safe. Moms protect kids, right?*

Cometh the hammer. The next thing I heard was "How dare you say such things about him! He loves you. You are his favorite, you know." She continued her berating rant. I looked up and our eyes locked. "Don't you dare say anything like that about him to anyone. He is the chief of police. Do you hear me? I never want to hear this again!" And I was sent off to my room. At that moment, an unseen gavel was dropped, and the sentence was brought down: *I was a liar.*

I was not prepared for my mother's defensive, angry reaction. I had hoped she would respond with words of assurance, telling me I had done the right thing in coming to her, and she would make sure I was safe. That day, a gulf of silence a mile wide was created between us.

That was the day I lost my voice. Not literally, though it felt like it. My mother's words felt like a punch in my stomach, putting a hole in the very layer of protection that I had created to defend myself against more pain. I felt like a truckload of salt was dumped on my open wounded heart. I remember walking as fast as I could down the hall to my room, hoping to get there before the tears spilled down my cheeks. I felt like I couldn't breathe, and life as I had known it had stopped. Her words echoed in my head while the sting of shame and the suffocating grip of judgment and condemnation seared my heart. A wave of shame now drowned my hope. Mother and daughter would pretend as if that conversation had never happened.

My world seemed to shift that day to being a colorless place. It was not black and white, just dull; grayish maybe. There were no clear-cut outlines, no vision of purpose or plans. My yesterdays, today, and tomorrows froze together like ice. I sat in the corner of my room, cold and shaking. It was an inside cold, not a cold that could be replaced with the warmth of a blanket or a hug. I felt abandoned, terrified and lost. Now I knew it wouldn't be over. The chief would continue. I felt like I had been accused of lying, but I had told the raw truth. In my courageous little girl attempt to expose something shameful, *I was shamed.*

At that moment, all I wanted was for my mom to believe me, but she didn't. I looked up toward the window but couldn't really see clearly. The tears diffused the light and confused the source of that light. I wanted to be frozen in time. I knew what all my yesterdays had been, and today held the mirror of many tomorrows reflecting that which already was; over and over again.

I remember asking God if He was there that day, and if He *was* there, did He care? I wondered if He was punishing me by not letting me know He was there. *"How long, O Lord? Will You forget me forever? How long will You hide Your face from me? How long must I wrestle with my thoughts and every day have sorrow in my heart?"* (Psalm 13:1-2).

I didn't want to cry, but I felt hollow. As the tears welled up, everything seemed to be coated with Vaseline; blurred, as if I were wearing an old person's thick reading glasses. Almost immediately, the floodgates opened, and I cried until there were no more tears. I don't remember the rest of that day, or even that week. I felt as if I was being swallowed up by a slimy pit from which there was no escape. Not only was my secret shame exposed, but now I was banished to a prison of rejection. Not just a rejection of my words, but a rejection of the validation my little girl heart needed.

Over the years, I would learn that when handled poorly, life's hurts can strip us of our inner voice, the very voice that God put within each of us to be able to speak for truth. If I had not had this experience, I may never have learned the value and power of the voice He instilled in me. Sometimes it is in losing that we find even more than we lost.

The abuse continued for two more long years until I was eleven. I can't tell you how or why it stopped. Even though in actuality it did end, I was never sure that it was over. I lived with the looming possibility that there would be more. All I know is that after a certain point in time, I was never taken to the chief's house again. He did, however, occasionally attend cocktail parties and gatherings hosted by my parents at our house. On these evenings, I would strategically banish myself to my room. Survival.

As a result of being forced to be silent when I wanted to speak, I learned that we cannot be true to ourselves or true to others if we adhere to the "rules" of shame. The little girl who lost her voice that day was robbed of a sense of self that only God could restore. It isn't always words that shut us down; sometimes it's the tone of those words, or a harsh look. Sometimes we lose our voice because the person who speaks the words to silence us is a trusted, loved, significant person in our lives. Sometimes we lose our voice in fear. Whatever the cause, the result is a horrific reality: we dare not speak up, or else.

I emphasize this because God never intended for any of us to lose our ability to speak. Rather, He gifted us with the ability to carry a message, His message; strong, loud and clear. When the enemy of our souls, the devil himself, can use something or someone to steal our voice, we become timid; we lose our sense of self-worth and we lose our capacity to see life with clarity. I became emotionally paralyzed that day, more so it seems than the abuse itself. I can't explain why, but what the chief did to me seemed less traumatic than not being believed by my mom when I tried to expose his abuse. This happens to victims of sexual abuse more often than we know. Not being believed brings more shame, and validates our feeling of somehow being responsible for the abuse. We shut down.

Evidently my mom didn't want to believe the abuse had occurred, so we both tiptoed around my reality. I couldn't talk about it and she wouldn't. It was there, but not there. I wished I had never spoken about it at all. When the abuse actually ended, the poisonous effects lingered; leaving ugly deposits of continued shame, increased self-consciousness, dread, fear, confusion, and isolation. Childhood sexual abuse affects the child's sense of peace and safety. I felt neither.

Grace Like Rain from His Word:

*"Come, My shy and modest dove — leave your seclusion, come out in the open. Let Me see your face, **let Me hear your voice**"* (Song of Solomon 2:14 MSG, emphasis mine).

I love the picture of this verse as our beloved Lord calls us out of isolation. He knows us completely and accepts us unconditionally. This truth helped me to realize that even though shame insisted I hide, Jesus was calling me forth, yearning to hear my voice. What we say to the Lord is precious and important to Him. This was a tipping point for me. As God was raining truth on my heart, His grace made it possible for me to receive that truth. Grace makes possibilities out of life's impossibilities.

Decades later, after my mom gave her heart to the Lord (I'll share that miracle with you a little later), I found the courage to mention the chief again. This time, everything was different. God not only gave me the right words, but the heart to receive what my mom had to say. She apologized for how she reacted when I tried to expose the abuse. The soft look in her eyes melted my heart and I found myself filled with compassion. We cried together and loved on each other. God not only restored my voice, He taught me how to revisit a place of pain with grace, without shaming my mom. He filled my heart with forgiveness and did a beautiful work in our relationship.

He values what is on our hearts, and He wants to hear from us. Our heavenly Father really cares how we feel. He wants us to be open and vulnerable with Him. He wants us to voice our issues, fears, disappointments, and hurts. Bringing our pain into the light of God's love is our first step toward healing. He gives *Grace Like Rain* to those places where we may have lost our voice, restoring us to not only be able to speak for ourselves, but for others. *"Speak up for the people who have no voice"* (Proverbs 31:8 MSG).

Ultimately, when God brings healing into our lives, He uses our healing as evidence to others that what He has done for us, He can do for them. As I have shared how God restored my lost voice with others, it has brought hope and courage to women to trust God to do the same in their lives. This is another place where I can say that I am thankful for everything I have ever gone through, and forever grateful for God's faithfulness to rain His grace over my life.

chapter four

GRACE FOR SHAME. . . "NUN"-THELESS

S hame is one of the hardest pits to climb out of; even when we try, it has a way of wrapping its tentacles around the core of our identity. It is important, however, to face off with the sources of our shame so that God can send His *Grace Like Rain* on assignment. Shame is unique to each individual, and even though similar incidents may evoke various degrees of shame in different people, each person is a candidate for His healing power.

It is vital to recognize the entry points of shame, and though the abuse by the chief was a huge source of shame, there were many others. The experience of shame is like walking from a well-lit room into a dark one. I believe that once shame drives its sword through the heart, it becomes a place of access for future traumatic events to build on that shame base. Shame enters uninvited, settles in, and makes room for more of the same. This was true for me.

I want to share a few childhood experiences that contributed to my shame-based self-concept. Though each event happened to involve nuns, it is not my intent to dishonor them or other nuns. In fact, God has used several sisters to become cherished mentors in my adult life.

I attended Catholic schools through my elementary and high school years. My favorite thing about private school was the required uniform, and not for the reason most think. Many of my classmates liked it because it eliminated the question of what to wear each day. I liked it because it helped me blend in, unnoticed… or so I thought.

My first day of first grade was frightening, having just transferred from public school kindergarten to Catholic school. I felt like a little lamb being herded from room to room and down long hallways with high ceilings. I was in a fear-induced fog, and probably missed important information such as the location of the girls' bathrooms. At lunchtime, I found myself in the cafeteria line with my tray and an undeniable urgency to go to the elusive girls' room. The other first-graders were chatting all around me. I felt as if I was invisible because they talked around me, behind me, and in front of me, but not *to* me. I didn't know anyone, and I was too afraid to ask for directions to the girls' bathroom. Then the unthinkable happened. Before I knew it, I was standing in a puddle of my own making. Yup. It happened.

I was mortified. Before I could figure out what to do next, the kids were laughing and stepping back from me and the lake beneath my feet. They summoned my first grade teacher, who came over and promptly instructed the children to move along and proceed through the lunch line. The nun then pushed me aside, and mopped up my puddle with a pile of towels. They weren't even paper towels; they were kitchen towels.

She took my hand and ushered me out of the cafeteria, and by now I had the attention of what seemed like the entire room. The long black layers of her dress swished against me as she annoyingly rushed me to the girls' room; which was surprisingly close. *If only I had known. If only I had asked.* She flung the stall door open, pushed me inside and slammed the door. She ordered me to remove my panties and hand them under the door to her. I resisted, maintaining that I could not leave the bathroom without my underwear. She insisted that she would wash, dry, and return them to me before the end of the school day. I reluctantly cooperated and handed them over.

The nun brought me back to my classroom, which was now filled with all the other six-year-olds, and as I walked in, so did a shameful silence. I felt as if a cloud of disgraceful darkness hovered over my head as I took my seat. It was the longest afternoon ever. Near the end of the day my teacher left and returned with none other than my panties in her hands. She held them up in front of the entire class and told me to come to the front of the room to get them and to go put them on before the bell rang. I wanted to disappear. She tried to quiet the kids, but I could still hear the whispers, sneers, and giggles as I walked out the door and down the hallway.

Embarrassing situations, handled poorly, can lead to shame. I internalized a message that day which was birthed out of fear. My fear of asking for directions resulted in an embarrassing accident, for which I was shamed. To make matters worse, when my mom arrived at school to drive us home, the nun leaned into the car window and told her what had happened. Now my family knew. I not only took the incident home with me, I took an entire carload of ridicule. That was my *Shame Nun-theless Experience Number One.* This shame located itself in my little heart, acting as a magnet for future shame.

Shame Nun-theless Experience Number Two: On the last day of second grade, as I was walking to my mom's car, the nun that would be my third grade teacher that September called me over to her. I liked her and looked forward to being in her class. She said, "Before you can be in my third grade class in September, I want you to count all your freckles and bring me the number on a piece of paper." Seriously? Who counts freckles?

Over the summer, I repeatedly reminded my parents about her request. At the end of August, I insisted that I would not be allowed to return to school unless we counted all my freckles. On Labor Day weekend, my parents finally humored me. We had company and my mom invited everyone to gather around me. Each person was told to circle off an area of my arms, back, and legs with an ink pen, and then count the freckles within the circle. I was happy there were no ink circles on my face. My mom collected the numbers and gave me the total on a piece of paper. To this day I don't know if they honestly counted those freckles or just appeased me. I was relieved to have completed my summer assignment. My little piece of paper would be my ticket to enter third grade.

On the first day of school, there was nothing more important to me than presenting my carefully folded note to my new teacher. I was certain she would be proud of me. As I entered the classroom, I went straight to her desk with my delivery. She opened it, and upon inspection, asked me to explain the number. "It's how many freckles I have. Remember, you told me I couldn't come to your class unless I counted them all." I was starting to feel nervous. Had she forgotten? Surely not. She began to laugh. Now she had the attention of the entire class. Scoffing, she asked, "Diana, did you really think I was serious? Anyone would have known I was kidding! That was just a joke." But I *did* take her seriously, and I *didn't* know she was kidding.

The class started laughing, and for the next several days, the kids called me "freckle girl." Honestly, my freckles had never been an issue to me. I rather liked them. It was one of the ways I was just like my dad: we were both covered with freckles. Now my freckles seemed to stain me, making me different from the other kids. I didn't want to be different. I didn't even want to be noticed. I wanted to be invisible. Third grade: the year my freckles became a source of ridicule and shame. Third grade: the year of the chief. Ugh. I hated third grade.

Shame Nun-theless Experience Number Three: For some unknown reason, we were transferred to yet another Catholic school for the next three years. Even though I hadn't had the best experiences in my previous school, it had become familiar to me, and I did well academically. Getting A's was important in my family. Achieving, I could do; fitting in, not so much. It seemed like my comfort level was being invaded by new teachers, new classmates, and an entirely new routine. From day one, I had my mind made up: I was not going to like this school.

On the first day of fourth grade, the teacher walked back and forth through the rows of desks overseeing each student's writing style. This nun wore a big black belt at her waist, from which dangled a huge set of black beads, and she carried a thick worn ruler. To say she was intimidating would be an understatement. When she got to me, she stopped abruptly and said, "Diana, why are you writing with your left hand?" I stammered and squeaked out that I always wrote with my left hand. "We don't write with our left hand here." I said, "But I can't write with my other hand," and continued to hold my pencil in my left.

She snapped my left hand with her ruler and told me to put my pencil in my right hand and begin writing. She stood over me sternly scolding me as I tried, failed, tried, and failed again. Each time I put the pencil back in my left hand, she would hit my hand with her ruler. Finally, she sent the rest of the class out to recess and told me I would stay inside until I learned to write with the correct hand. What she didn't know was that I hated recess, and didn't mind missing it. I did mind being ridiculed in front of the other students. The two of us spent recess in the classroom. She hovered over me with disapproval while I tried to give it my best shot, but even my best wasn't good enough. For several days, she insisted that I write with my right hand. Each time my attempt failed, she would hit my hand with her nasty ruler.

I didn't like her, and I resented being hit for such a ridiculous reason. Over the next few months, I figured out how to keep writing with my left hand when she wasn't looking. I practiced at home for hours with my paper slanted so my writing would not betray that I was writing as a lefty. As she paced through the rows and came close to my desk, I would slip my pencil into my right hand. After she would pass by, I would turn my paper sideways and write with my left hand; righty-style. I don't know where I got the tenacity to keep writing left-handed. I do know that I just wanted her to leave me alone.

The shame around writing came as a result of being punished for something that came naturally to me. Writing as a left-hander seemed natural to me, yet it resulted in scolding, ridicule, and punishment. I couldn't understand why she was so angry with me. Children who are shamed often try to make sense of their disgrace. Unfortunately, there are some things that will never make sense.

Shame Nun-theless Experience Number Four: After three years, our parents moved us back to the first school where I had peed in the lunchroom and was humiliated for my freckle count. Yeh, *that* school. Now all the third graders had grouped off into cliques, and it seemed impossible for me to find a way to fit in with the kids.

The nun who was my seventh grade teacher was also the school dance instructor, so my mom decided I should take ballet. Graceful, I was not; which was likely the reason for my enrollment. At the end of the school year came the dreaded ballet recital. The teacher assigned all parts except two: a girl part and boy part. You guessed it. She then announced casually, "Diana will dance the part of the boy and Jackie will be the girl." I didn't want to be a boy. Remember? I was the girl my mom had hoped would be a boy. So here I was again. I was afraid to tell my ballet instructor that I didn't want to be a boy, so I divulged my distress to Jackie, who took it upon herself to broadcast it to the entire class.

One of the other students snarled, "Well, you look like a boy, so you should be the boy." That hit the pit of my stomach like a rock. *Really? I look like a boy?* I slowly, ashamedly, backed myself up against the wall as tears began to spill from my eyes. *No! Don't cry! You'll only draw attention to yourself!* Too late. Jackie saw me crying and told the teacher, "She's crying. I'll be the boy." Reluctantly, the dance instructor told me I would play the role of the girl. It was horrible. During the entire performance, I danced with Jackie, who hated being the boy. Now I not only felt ashamed for being a girl that looked like a boy, but I also felt guilty for receiving the part of the girl.

Shame Nun-theless Experience Number Five: That same seventh grade year I signed up for the girls' basketball team. The reason I joined was twofold: my dad wanted me to play, and there were no tryouts. I wasn't athletic at all, but I did want to please my dad. The three long years of the chief's abuse was over, and I welcomed something that might help me forget.

I had been sitting on the bench for the first month of our season and hadn't minded at all. Then one day, for various reasons, most of the team was absent. The main coach wasn't there either, so the assistant nun stepped up to take charge. To my dismay, she put me in the game.

Thankfully, the first half of the game was uneventful. Early in the second half, the score was tied, and the ball came toward me. I panicked, but reluctantly picked it up and began to dribble. To my surprise, there was no one near the basket, so I kept dribbling toward the hoop. I heard people screaming my name, and assumed they were cheering me on, so I kept dribbling. Down the court I went. I positioned myself under the basket and to my surprise, I scored! My excitement, however, was short-lived as the whistle blew, and the nun took me out of the game. All my teammates were angry with me. *I had just scored for the wrong team.*

The nun began to scold me, screaming that I probably cost the team the game. Apparently they had been calling my name to let me know that I had been dribbling the ball towards the other team's basket. My shining sports moment immediately became my most embarrassing. Needless to say, I was happy to sit on the bench for the rest of the season. I was the girl who shot for the wrong team. I felt so stupid and ashamed.

Shame Nun-theless Experience Number Six: That same summer, a friend and I got permission to volunteer at a Catholic orphanage a few miles away from my house. I think I gravitated toward the orphanage because I could relate to the children. Even though I had parents, I could identify with their feelings of not belonging. Helping out at the orphanage was appealing to me because it was a reason to be away from home, plus it gave me an opportunity to do something meaningful.

We went three times a week for four hours each day. Our direct supervisor was, of course, a nun. Each day she gave us our assignments and usually we were able to stay together. Our responsibilities included playground oversight, one-on-one time with the girls, helping with crafts, and reading to them. I looked forward to my days at the orphanage and spending time with the kids.

One Monday, several weeks after I started working there, I noticed that Jenny, a six-year-old, had become more withdrawn and was less interested in our group activities. When I asked what was wrong, the color drained from her face as her eyes filled with tears. She bolted to the corner of the room and curled up on the floor. Something was terribly wrong and I decided to keep an eye on her. For the next several days, I made myself available in case she wanted to talk to me.

A week later, when I arrived at the orphanage, I didn't see Jenny. When I asked about her, the nun said she was sick in bed. I made my way to her dorm room and found her hiding under her covers. I peeked in and asked if she needed me. No response. I sat on the floor next to her bed, and after about an hour, I began to hear sobs coming from under her blanket. After prodding, she told me that one of the nuns had been touching her inappropriately. I was enraged. When I asked if she had told anyone, she said she had been too afraid to talk about it. I knew that fear too well. I held her and rocked her until the sobbing stopped.

I finally asked the tough question: "Jenny, will you let me tell someone what has been happening? What she is doing to you is not okay. It's wrong. Please let me help." She was shaking now, and told me she was afraid she would get in trouble. I told her she didn't do anything wrong, but now I was in a dilemma. I got in trouble when I told my mother about the chief. I couldn't promise that she wouldn't get in trouble. I couldn't even promise that the abuse would stop. I knew from experience that the chief's abuse continued for two years after I told my mom. Now I was trying to do for her what I hadn't been able to do for myself. I wanted to get her out of there, but I knew I couldn't. All I could do was offer to notify someone who *could* help. She finally agreed.

When I finished my duties for the day, I took the long walk down the hallway to the main office. I muttered that I needed to speak to the sister who was in charge of volunteers. She invited me in, and I proceeded to tell her what Jenny had told me. Her demeanor immediately changed; it was as if she had taken off one mask and put on another. When I had arrived, she was kind, welcoming and sweet. Now she was stern, angry, and authoritative. I could feel my legs trembling. She stood up abruptly and walked me all the way outside, to the edge of the property.

On the bus ride home, I second-guessed my decision to report Jenny's story. I wondered whether my telling would make things better or worse for Jenny. After getting off the bus, I used the mile-long walk down the hill to my house to consider different scenarios in my mind. *Maybe Jenny would get to sleep in a different dorm room. Perhaps the nun who had been touching her would be fired. Maybe the next time I would see Jenny, she would be happy again.*

Before I knew it, I was walking up the steps to my house. My mother, all red-in-the-face, met me at the front door to inform me that the orphanage had called requesting that I not return. I was horrified. I insisted on explaining what had happened, but she excused me, convinced that she had all the information she needed. She reamed me out with a list of ways I had disappointed her, and dismissed me before I could speak, reminding me that I should be ashamed of myself for embarrassing her and causing so much trouble at the orphanage.

I was indeed ashamed. I had blown it big time. The nuns would not allow me to go back to the orphanage.

From that point on, my friend was never put in a group with Jenny, so there was no way to check on her. Ugh. I felt horrible that in my effort to help Jenny, I had actually let her down. Through many attempts, I could not follow up on little Jenny. To this day, when she comes to mind, I pray for her.

Shaming experiences like these sliced against my sense of worth, contributing to my poor self-esteem and hopeless pessimism. We convince ourselves that we get what we deserve which only adds to the garbage heap of yesterday's lies. We can either play it safe, accept what is, and stay stuck in the mold of the past; or we can allow God's *Grace Like Rain* to transform us by helping us to renew our mind according to His Truth.

I had to face off with the lies I believed about myself as a result of the tsunami of shame that swallowed me. I was drowning in shame, but I had no clue how to get free; in fact, I didn't even know whether freedom was possible. There was a war going on inside of me. A battle between the old and the new. Old beliefs versus new beliefs. Old habits of thinking versus new habits of thinking. I knew that if I was going to replace old patterns of thinking, God would have to shower me with grace to learn His Word.

I have always loved being a student. I loved to learn, and I loved to study. However, I spent a lot of energy in classes in a fervent dash for the right answer to every question the teachers asked. Not knowing the answers not only brought unwanted negative attention to me, but it also surfaced embarrassment and shame. I believe God put the love for learning in me. His *Grace Like Rain* converted that into a love for studying the Truth of His Word.

My assignment was huge, and impossible without the grace of God. I needed to let go of my faulty beliefs, and replace them with the infallible Truth of His uncondi- tional love and acceptance. My feelings of inferiority kept me from feeling worthy of pursuing my healing. Shame breeds inferiority, inadequacy, and low self-esteem. I had come to His saving grace, but now I had to accept and believe God's Truth on a personal level. He doesn't call us by our shame; He calls us by our name. He doesn't call us by what we have done, or by what we have gone through; He calls us by whose we are: HIS!

Grace Like Rain from His Word:

As a daughter of God, I have no reason to feel ashamed. This truth has motivated me in my journey toward healing. As I believe and accept God's Word, my understanding of the truth that He values me continues to grow. In order to come out of the darkness of the lies I had come to believe, I needed to allow God's *Grace Like Rain* to pour these truths over me:

- *"Since you have heard about Jesus and have learned the truth that comes from Him, throw off your old sinful nature and your former way of life, which is corrupted by lust and deception. Instead, let the Spirit renew your thoughts and attitudes. Put on your new nature, created to be like God—truly righteous and holy"* (Ephesians 4:21-24 NLT).
- *"I have been crucified with Christ and I no longer live, but Christ lives in me. The life I live in the body, I live by faith in the Son of God, who loved me and gave Himself for me"* (Galatians 2:20).
- *"Now there is no condemnation for those who belong to Christ Jesus"* (Romans 8:1 NLT).
- *"Therefore, if anyone is in Christ, he is a new creation; the old has gone, the new has come!"* (2 Corinthians 5:17).

- *"In all these things we are more than conquerors through Him who loved us"* (Romans 8:37).
- *"For we are God's workmanship, created in Christ Jesus to do good works, which God prepared in advance for us to do"* (Ephesians 2:10).
- *"God began doing a good work in you, and I am sure He will continue it until it is finished"* (Philippians 1:6 NCV).

I clung to God's promise that He would continue the work He began in me. This promise didn't include any contingency clauses dependent on my getting it right or doing it right. It was His work in my life. He began it, and I had every hope that what He began, He would finish.

chapter five

OUR LIFE STORY POSITIONS US FOR GRACE

I know I am midstream in sharing my story, but before we go too far I want to make sure you understand that your life is a story as well, and it is important. Each person's story is unique. Unique, but not isolated. Your life story and mine are designed to intersect, connect, and create something new when they come together. Telling my story is bittersweet. I feel blessed to invite you into my journey to share with you the many ways God has rained His grace on my life. On the other hand, I miss out on *your* story. I don't get to meet the cast of characters, follow the twists and turns of the events of your life, or share in your significant God-moments.

I hope you realize that God is actively involved in *your* story. As you continue to read mine, remember that whether your story is currently stuck on drama, moving through change, tangled in a confusing plot, or invaded by what seem to be alien characters; God has a plan for you, and His plan is good. Your life is intended to count for something, and your story is meant to impact lives.

Be patient; you and your story are positioned for His abundant grace.

The truth is, there are no coincidences, no accidents, and no surprises to God. Everything we go through is intentionally woven into our story to make something known about God. As people come into our lives, hopefully they will discover more of God's character, His faithfulness, His goodness, and His love. As they observe our unfolding story, they will see His plan and purpose come into focus. At first they may only see our brokenness, much like the fragmented glass pieces in the bottom of a kaleidoscope. They will also see what happens as God's grace causes the cylinder to turn, transforming brokenness into something beautiful. He shows up right in the middle of the imperfect novel of our life, pours out His grace, and transforms us. He then uses our story to demonstrate His goodness and love to a world that is desperate to know Him and be known by Him. Simply put, God loves to put His grace on display through our story.

I grew up not daring to dream for a life that counted. I felt like every dream I may have secretly held in my heart was short-circuited by the circumstances of my life. Those of us who endured the violation of childhood sexual abuse may have allowed the light to go out on our dreams. When I realized that God knew every event of my life before I was even born, it gave me hope. My hope evolved into faith as I accepted the truth that He was not only at the beginning of my life in creating me, but He stands at the edge of eternity drawing me into the destiny He has for me.

When I first received this truth, I felt life flow through me in a new way. I mattered. My life mattered. He authors my life story and invites me to co-author with Him. I love being a part of His unfolding plan for me. There was one condition, however; I needed to cooperate with His will for my life. I had to learn to bring my mind, will, and emotions in line with His Word. That faced me off with a Grand Canyon-sized hole in my heart that had to be healed.

My role as co-author was not only to allow God to do His work in me, but to work with Him in the process. I discovered that no matter what we have gone through, His love graces over our lives, rewriting the scenes that were intended to be destructive. I'm not insinuating that God pretends abuse didn't happen. It's better than that. He takes each painful experience, sets it up against the backdrop of His plan for our lives, and it becomes something new.

So where was I. . . oh yeah, a teenager in high school. On most days, when the final bell rang, I hurried from campus to make my way home to help with the kids. Even though I believed that my life carried no value; taking care of my younger siblings brought me joy. I often retreated to my room with my journals, books, art, and music. I learned to get lost in what I considered were my safe havens. I wanted to forget the unforgettable. I would write like crazy in my journals when my mind was so full that I thought it would explode. I would use pencils and pastels to release what I couldn't put into words. I would read novels and lose myself in someone else's story. I would write fiction and let myself dream of living through my writing. I withdrew into a self-imposed exile; a place where I could disappear in secret. When I thought of my future, I was often haunted by despair. Sometimes music helped to drown out the inescapable war zone within me.

One of my escapes was in Simon and Garfunkel's song: *I Am A Rock*, because the lyrics rang out what I could not voice.

I Am A Rock – Simon and Garfunkel (from album *Sounds of Silence*, released 1966)

A winter's day in a deep and dark December;
I am alone,
Gazing from my window to the streets below
On a freshly fallen silent shroud of snow.
I am a rock, I am an island.

I've built walls, a fortress deep and mighty,
That none may penetrate.
I have no need of friendship; friendship causes pain.
It's laughter and it's loving I disdain.
I am a rock, I am an island.

Don't talk of love, I've heard the words before;
It's sleeping in my memory.
I won't disturb the slumber of feelings that have died.
If I never loved I never would have cried.
I am a rock, I am an island.

I have my books and my poetry to protect me;
I am shielded in my armor,
Hiding in my room, safe within my womb.
I touch no one and no one touches me.
I am a rock, I am an island.

And a rock feels no pain;
And an island never cries.

Getting lost in these lyrics did two things for me: first, they put a voice to my pain, and second, they validated my isolation. The more I played the song (I wore out two records), the more I wanted to be that rock, that island. After all, rocks and islands had no feelings, so they couldn't be hurt. *Being shielded in armor sure sounded safe to me.*

Each year of high school brought increasing evidence that my parents' marriage would soon end in divorce. We walked a tightrope between the arguments and the cold silence as we treaded carefully around the proverbial elephant in the living room. When it was quiet, an eerie stillness would hover amidst the thick tense atmosphere. No one, however, dared ask the question, "What's going on?" As hard as parents try to portray to their children that the family is intact when it's crumbling moment by moment, kids figure it out. We weren't stupid; we knew our family was in trouble.

At the end of my junior year, my classmates were looking forward to our last year of high school, but I just wanted time to stop. A friend dragged me to the final dance of the year; the last place I wanted to be. Classmates were dancing all around me while I stood awkwardly in a spot where I hoped no one would notice me. I felt a sense of relief when the music came to an abrupt end. I thought the dance was over, and I could finally go home. I just wanted to get out of there.

I soon found out that the dance *wasn't* over. One band was going on break while the second band was starting their first song. *Ugh. This night was never going to end.* Then it happened. Enter Mike. God's *Grace Like Rain* was positioning me for my future. A sweaty, carefree, bouncy drummer came over during his band's break, flashed his all-American-boy smile at me, and asked me to dance. How could I refuse? He was super cute, adorably shy, and very polite. This was going to be the first dance of the rest of my life. Unknown to me at the time, four years later I would be his bride.

This new relationship was to me like a life raft on rough waters. I began to learn that Mike was trustworthy, safe, and kind. Over the summer of 1968, he became the companion I didn't know I needed, and we became best friends long before we fell in love. God knew it had to happen that way. He knew I needed to grow in trust and take my protective walls down, in order to know others and be known. Mike listened, and valued what I shared with him. He never called me a nut case and never judged me or my family.

God knew that Mike was the perfect choice for me, and His grace placed me at that dance. My heavenly Father loved me that night by introducing me to the one who would become the love of my life. Over the next few months, I would come to appreciate so many qualities in this young man. He was thoughtful, attentive, and affirming. He had the ability to look me eyeball-to-eyeball and not so much as flinch when I would share what was going on inside me. He excelled at listening, and it was most endearing to me when I didn't want answers and only wanted to be heard.

On the home front, things were getting worse. The tension in the house was thick, and our family was like a colony of ants. Everyone came and went, scurrying from where they were to where they needed to be, but no one talked about the real issues. My dad began to worry about me and enrolled me in a Dale Carnegie Course with several of the men who worked for his business. *Dale Carnegie: How to Win Friends and Influence People.* Are you kidding me, Dad? I didn't want *friends* and the only people I wanted to *influence* were those who could get me out of taking this ridiculous course. Bless his heart. I now know that he was only trying to toss me a lifejacket to keep me from drowning.

To be the good, compliant daughter, I took the course to appease my dad. I was a sixteen-year-old amidst a class of people with gray hair. I think they felt sorry for me each time it was my turn to give the dreaded, tormenting, weekly speeches. To make matters worse, one of my classmates (a woman, I might add), *died* during the weeks of the course. I remember crying, sweating, turning red with embarrassment, and shaking in the knees every time I had to give my required speech. Many years later, my dad agreed that enrolling me in the Dale Carnegie Course at that time was probably not the best idea.

That summer, in his continued concern for me, my dad decided to send me to Florida to stay with my cousins for two weeks. I know he meant well; I was a mess. Honestly, the last thing I wanted was to leave home. As chaotic as it was at home, my room was still my refuge, and my growing friendship with Mike had become a new source of strength to me. *Father Knows Best,* and off I went. I was absolutely miserable. As much as my cousins did their best to show me a good time, I called my dad every day in tears pleading to come home. Mike wrote me regularly, which made me want to come home all the more. Eventually, my dad gave in and allowed me to return home a few days early.

Things had escalated with my parents and just three weeks after I got back, my mom divorced my dad, remarried, and left Vermont with the three youngest kids. I was lost. I cried so hard it felt as if my heart was going to explode. The pain of abandonment felt like it was sucking the life right out of me. I wanted to stop time. A few days later, my dad introduced us to the woman he would marry in less than two weeks.

My mom had just left and now we were getting a new mom. *Did we even want a new mom?* No matter how hard I tried, I couldn't wrap my brain around this transition. Dad tried to soften the blow by promising that everything would be better assuring us that our home would be happy and we would forget the past. At the same time, he instructed us to never refer to our real mother as "mom." That title had been transferred to our stepmother. Before long, any reference to our real mom disappeared from our dialogue.

It was as if one curtain closed on our family unit, and my dad opened another to reveal our new and improved family. I was completely devastated and confused. Exit: mom and three siblings; a girl and two boys. Enter: stepmother and three new siblings; also a girl and two boys. Shortly after their wedding it became obvious that my relationship with my dad was about to change dramatically.

I should add that since my mom gave birth to a baby every other year, the older siblings were assigned the responsibility of helping with the younger ones. Caring for the three youngest kids, ages 2, 4, and 6, had been one of the few things that brought me joy. When I was with them, I felt a playfulness and lighthearted ease. This made it even more devastating when my mom left with the three little ones. I felt like my own kids had been torn away from me. Not only were they gone, but now they were out of state and out of touch. I sank into despair. My life was a nightmare and I couldn't wake up.

My dad had come to depend on me during the year surrounding the divorce. It felt good to know that he needed me to cook, shop, and assist with the children. Now dad had someone else to fill that role; he had a new wife. We kids, on the other hand, had just lost three siblings and gained three new ones. There was no buffer time allowing us to grieve the family we had lost, and adjust to the family we had gained. Our home life shifted dramatically. I not only felt displaced, I felt fragmented; as if part of my heart had been ripped out. I survived at home by going through the motions and made it through my senior year by focusing on grades, graduation and college plans.

Grace Like Rain from His Word:

"And we know that in all things God works for the good of those who love Him, who have been called according to His purpose" (Romans 8:28).

"But the Lord has become my fortress, and my God the rock in whom I take refuge" (Psalm 94:22).

Each chapter of our life story invites a new measure of God's grace. A shattering of earthquake-like proportions had hit my life, my home, and my family. I would learn later that God never took His eyes off of me, and that He had perfectly positioned me for His grace. I was confused, depressed and heartbroken; but positioned, nonetheless. I share this because even when we do not know that we are positioned for an invasion of grace, we are. Even when we cannot see God doing anything good in our midst, He is. He is faithful. He truly does work all things together for our good. He takes the devastating events of our lives and dips them in His vat of grace, transforming them into His work of art.

God used this powerful verse in my life: "*Is not My Word like fire," declares the Lord, "and like a hammer that breaks a rock in pieces?*" (Jeremiah 23:29). I had decided that becoming "hard as a rock" worked for me. I had needed safety, and thought I had found it by isolating myself. Isolation isn't safety where God is concerned. He used the power of His Word to break my protective rock-like fortification, teaching me that true safety can only be found in relationship with the Lord. He used the Truth of His Word to crush my false sense of security, and in doing so, He exposed me to His love and grace. As always, my heavenly Father knew exactly what I needed.

To this day I can still quote the words to that Simon and Garfunkel song. Now, my memory has been graced-over. I no longer need to be a rock. I have come to know and love Jesus Christ, the true Rock. I have no need to be a fortress, for the Lord has become my fortress, and the One in whom I take refuge.

chapter six

GRACE UNRECOGNIZED

I love how God works. Regardless of what we go through in our lives, He has seen our end from the beginning and nothing trumps His plan. Not abuse, betrayal, divorce, loss, trauma. Nothing. No event takes Him by surprise and He fully sees in advance how He will bring redemption to our mess. He knew what I would go through as a little girl. He knew I would *be* a little girl. Even when I wasn't aware, His *Grace Like Rain* was being poured across my entire life. He has a purpose for each one of us and nothing can thwart that purpose.

My family was Catholic, and we attended church every week. I took Mass very seriously because it was a constant in my life. I knew God existed, and I enjoyed hearing the priest teach us more about Him. I believed in God and hoped to make it to heaven at the end of my life. I thought that my soiled history would cost me a little time in Purgatory, but hey, that seemed like a small price to pay for eternal safety.

In Catholicism, Purgatory is a place of purification through suffering after death. Catholics believe in the necessity of reparation for sins, even after forgiveness.

This is considered justice for having offended God. That made perfect sense to me as a child. After all, I was damaged; so Purgatory was the deal God offered people like me. My concept of heaven was that it was a final forever place of safety and freedom from pain. I did, however, always secretly wonder if God could heal my brokenness and make something worthwhile out of me.

My relationship with Mike grew and got stronger. We both knew that our friendship had grown into love, and we spoke of engagement and marriage. Our conversations were less centered on my survival and more focused on our future. I still felt broken and lost on the inside, but Mike brought me joy. It felt good to feel good. My sadness at home seemed to fade into the backdrop of my dream that one day I would leave and begin a new life with my husband.

I was eighteen when Mike's fifteen-year-old sister, Becky, had a dramatic conversion in her life. She was aglow with the love of Jesus. Several times each week she would visit me at the ferry dock snack bar where I worked the summer before my second year of college. It seemed as if every time I looked up she was there, waiting to talk to me about Jesus, and pleading with me to go to Bible study with her. No matter what we would be talking about, she always found a way to bring the conversation back around to God.

I finally told Mike that I was going to accept her invitation just to get her off my back. He encouraged me to go because she had been hounding him also. Deep down inside I had a flicker (just a flicker) of hope that Jesus could do for me what He had done for Becky. On the evening of August 1, 1970, as I walked into the hair salon where the ladies gathered for Bible study, I had no idea what God had in store for me. *Would I leave the same way I had arrived? Would I simply be relieved that Becky would finally leave me alone?* I was about to encounter God's *Grace Like Rain.*

My guard was definitely up as I walked into the salon. The room was crowded, and this was one time I was secretly hoping that there would be no chair for me. Several gracious women kindly offered me their seats. It was as if they were expecting me. My guard slowly dropped as it became evident that they were happy to have me join them. As the evening transitioned from prayer to sharing to Bible reading and discussion, one thing stood out to me: there was a remarkable peace in every voice and on every face. Some women spoke of what Jesus was doing in their lives, and how He had answered various prayers; while others asked for prayer for other issues. It was evident that these women loved Jesus and they had an obvious assurance of His love for them.

The rest of the night was a blur. I snapped out of my fog when we were told to bow our heads. I heard the Bible study leader's words: "Jesus cares about each one of us. He died not only to forgive us, but also so we could build a relationship with Him, learn to love Him, and spend eternity with Him in heaven. Does anyone here want to know Jesus as their personal Savior and Lord?" I had never heard that terminology. As I considered the possibility that I was too far gone for God's love and forgiveness to reach me, the leader shut down my thoughts as if I had voiced them out loud and spoke of His mercy and grace.

Did she say *relationship? Personal Savior and Lord? Did* she say *I could learn to love Him and go to heaven with Him?* This was an offer that sounded too good to be true. Reverse gravity pulled my hand toward the ceiling and the room filled with the sound of applause. *Hey! I thought everyone's eyes were closed!* Unknown to me, these women had my salvation at the top of their prayer list. Becky jumped up, came over to me, and soon I was swarmed by a full-on group hug. We stayed late into the night, and I sat like a hungry puppy in the midst of adoring pet-lovers.

These wonderful women answered every question I asked, and directed me to passages in the new Bible they presented to me. I didn't know much about the Bible but now I couldn't wait to read it. I took the suggestions of the women at the Bible study to start in the New Testament with the gospel of John. That evening, Jesus changed my life forever. God used the internal battle raging within me to reveal my need for Him. I left filled with hope, peace, and newfound joy. God showed up in such a powerful manner; there was no way I could doubt His love for me.

I went home and couldn't go to sleep. I wrote in my journal and read the entire book of John for the very first time in my very first Bible. I couldn't put it down. I had an unquenchable thirst for the truth about God's love for me as every word found its way into my parched heart. The good news was that He loved me. Period. No strings attached.

Growing up in my neighborhood church, I had been taught that God loved me and sent His Son to die for me. I knew that if I put my trust in Him as my Savior, I would go to heaven. I had always felt as if I was just one of the multitudes for whom Jesus had died. But this night was different. Something came alive inside of me. *This was personal.* That night I came to know that God had a plan and purpose for my life and I was not just one in a multitude. I was chosen, special, valued and loved. I learned that heaven was not only my eternal destination but that God had a destiny for me, and I became alive with hope and expectation as I began to embark on this journey of discovery.

One of the first Scripture verses I learned was, *"Anyone who belongs to Christ has become a new person. The old life is gone; a new life has begun"* (2 Corinthians

5:17 NLT). I loved the possibility of this verse but struggled with applying it to my own life. Although I believed I was spiritually new, I was still plagued with the residual impact of my old life. I had a hard time reconciling the old Diana with the new. I found myself suspended between the past and my spiritual transformation, and couldn't find balance. I would attend the Bible study, learn truth from God's Word, yet within a few days I would sink back into despair.

I expected my new faith in Christ to erase my pain, shame, fears, and everything else that was wrong with me. I discovered I wasn't going to have a quick fix, but rather, healing that would take time, prayer, and surrender. I needed to step over into a realm that had been defiled: trust. I needed to trust God with my heart and my life. I decided to invite His Truth to become my truth: *"Trust in the Lord with all your heart and lean not on your own understanding; in all your ways acknowledge Him and He will make your paths straight"* (Proverbs 3:5-6).

I experienced God's grace in that decision. As I surrendered my reluctance and fear to Him, He poured His *Grace Like Rain* over me and washed me with new hope. When we lack grace from earthly relationships, it is often difficult to believe that we can receive grace from God. But I was raising the white flag. I was surrendering to the gift of God's grace, unaware of just how far His grace would reach into my life. God has an unending capacity to forgive and a limitless ability to restore. He sees us as worthy, regardless of our behavior. He loves us simply because we are His children. Yes, He commands us to obey Him, He desires that we love Him, trust Him, and communicate with Him; but His love for us has always been ahead of our response to Him.

For the next year, I faithfully attended those Bible studies with Becky. I was filled with a new hunger to know God, and the ladies were amazingly patient in teaching me. My love for God's Word was growing daily. Every page seemed to bring answers, questions, more answers, and more questions. Becky went from being an annoying fifteen year old who wouldn't give up on her crusade to bring me to Jesus, to a special friend for whom I will be eternally grateful. Almost exactly one year after my life-changing encounter with God in the hair salon, Becky suffered an aneurism and went home to be with the Lord at age sixteen. This young lady impacted so many people through her short life, and even more in her home-going.

I am forever inspired by Becky's relentless pursuit of me, and I am constantly aware that each of us is on this planet for a purpose. It is our responsibility to discover that purpose and step into it, as well as to help others come to recognize that they too have a destiny. Becky was God's gift of *grace unrecognized* to me. Ever since, I have asked God to give me eyes to see His gift of grace in each person's life. I want to recognize Him in every way possible, and I want to be used to bring God's gift of grace to others.

Grace Like Rain from His Word:

"No eye has seen, no ear has heard, no mind has conceived what God has prepared for those who love Him" (1 Corinthians 2:9).

We have no idea what God has in store for us. What matters is that He does. And it's good. I never would have imagined that my fiancé's sister would be the vessel God would use to introduce me to His grace, and would then be gone from our lives only months later. I believe with all my heart that Becky was compelled with a sense of urgency for the King and His Kingdom. She was purposed and focused. She was determined and relentless. She had eyes to see, and ears to hear.

Back in the seventies, we used to sing a song that captured the essence of how I felt. I don't remember the artist, but there was one line that is so true of my salvation experience: "When I wasn't even looking He found me." I really wasn't looking for Jesus, but He was looking for me. He wasn't looking to harm me, correct me, or list everything wrong with me. He pursued me because He loved me. He found me because I was lost. What a wonderful Savior! I am so thankful that He used Becky to introduce me to Himself. She told me that she didn't know why she kept pestering me, but I now know it was God's grace seeking me out. Not only was I deeply loved by God, but I soon learned that *I am His child!* Now I was about to discover my true Father-daughter relationship.

chapter seven

GRACE FOR SECRET DESIRES OF THE HEART

"Lord, all my desire is before You;
my sighing is not hidden from You."
Psalm 38:9 NKJV

As we travel through my grace discovery, you will notice that these chapters are not a smooth journey, but rather pit stops along the way to visit grace places. There are many, and I feel it's important to point them out as we go. Don't worry; we'll catch up with the story line. One of my favorite grace moments was discovering that God has always been aware of the secret longings and desires of my heart. This is significant for me because as a child I was afraid to desire the cool stuff because I felt unworthy. To me, cool stuff included things like having a trusted friend, falling in love, getting married, having a family; normal stuff like what the neighbors had; what my classmates had; what I saw on TV shows like *Leave it to Beaver, Father Knows Best,* and *My Three Sons.* Nice families. Happy people. Deep within, I held my secret

73

longings close to my heart, hoping that they weren't too good to be true.

My dream to marry Mike and spend the rest of my life with him was definitely one of those *I hope it's not too good to be true* desires. I went to sleep every night wondering if it would still be true when I woke up the next morning. Mike and I still talk about the "baggage" I brought into our marriage as a result of my childhood. Later on I will share with you some of the hurdles we faced, but I will say this: there was no hurdle too high for God's grace to overcome. I am so thankful that it is God who puts good desires in our hearts.

In hindsight I realize that in spite of what my childhood was like, woven through the pages of my earliest diaries and journals were the now obvious threads of passion and desire. Not just for freedom from pain, but to walk in true liberty. Not just to discover my identity, but to have a life that counts for something. God has put His grace strength within each of us not only to carry us through difficult situations, or enable us to endure personal trauma, but also to lead us into those things He has destined for our futures. I share this because too often I think we shrink back from great expectations for our future because of great devastation in our past.

God wants to reconnect us to His original design in creating us. *"So God created man in His own image, in the image of God He created him; male and female He created them"* (Genesis 1:27). Because we were created in the image of the Creator, we have amazing potential on every level. I believe that at the core of His act in creating us, God put within each one of us a longing to live as we were created to live; in spite of our sins, the sins against us, or life in general.

It is important to note that our belief system has a lot to do with our longings. If my belief system is faulty, my longings will be clouded by a limited perspective. As I allow my belief system to be touched by God's grace, my longings and desires will be more pleasing to Him. When my desires actually find their purpose in bringing God pleasure, I find joy in the journey toward that desired goal. Unfortunately, when we dwell on our pain, disappointments, and unmet expectations; we act and react out of our emotions, without taking the time to consider what God might value.

God showers His *Grace Like Rain* over our disappointments, crushed hopes, and unmet expectations, bringing fresh possibility for us to rise out of the ashes and run into our destiny. I know this is true because it is precisely what He has done in my life and in the lives of so many others. This is the reason I have taken a detour in the middle of my story. I want you to know that there is grace for your secret longings. As you move with me through these next chapters, allow God's grace to reawaken any hope that may have gone to sleep, and allow Him to help you recapture any dream that may have been aborted. No matter how far you feel from your hopes and dreams, God's grace can still take you there.

Opening our hearts to God's grace is not a quick-fix solution. Just having awareness doesn't make everything that seems wrong, become right. None of us will be completely free from pain until we are in heaven. But if we respond to grace as God applies it to our circumstances we will see His living work in our lives and then join in what He is doing and where He is taking us. The grace ride is much more exciting when we remember three things: God is in control; He wants our life to be restored more than we do, and He gives grace for the process.

I had several longings that seemed out of reach for me, including: the longing for a reconnection with my mother and three siblings, the longing for marriage and family,

and especially – the longing to matter. When I felt courageous, I gave way to these longings and allowed myself to
dream of rising above my past. I wanted to discover and
live out my real purpose. The fact that I even felt a sense
of courage was grace-driven, not Diana-driven.

Our secret longings, desires, and passions fuel our
movement through life. When God helped me identify
the deepest desires of my heart, I discovered that they
included significance, purpose, wholeness, freedom,
and value. Grace awakened me to longings I wasn't even
aware of; longings that God put deep within me. These
included a longing to be known without feelings of shame,
a longing for intimacy with Him, and a longing to discover
my true identity. All I knew was that God was stirring an
awareness of His good plans for my future.

Longing to be Known by God

It is one thing to desire to grow in our knowledge
of God, but it is an entirely different thing to long to be
known *by* Him. The first time I was introduced to this
possibility, it seemed like fingernails scraping across a
chalkboard. It grated against my precautionary sense
of self. It seemed safe for me to grow in my *knowledge
of Him*, maybe because I could decide just how much I
wanted to know Him and then set my own pace. *Control.*
However, when it came to allowing Him to access my
heart in intimacy, it seemed too much like an invasion at
first, and I wasn't sure that I was ready.

I knew it would mean my protective walls would
need to go, and I would be unveiled before Him. God
wanted me to love Him without holding anything back.
He wanted our relationship to be based on transparency,
honesty, and truth. But that would mean He would see
the really ugly shameful places, and that horrified me.

Ultimately, it was slamming into my need for protection and safety.

In principle, I knew that God knew everything about me. After all, He was God. But that didn't mean I was extending an invitation for Him to walk around in all my dark places. The thought of a holy God messing around in the rubble of my past made me recoil. I wanted God to have my life, but did we really have to visit the worst of me?

The longing to be known by God eventually won out as I realized it was another place for grace. Once again, His Word torpedoed my logic. He continuously showed me in Scripture how He has always known me and has always loved me. He especially used Psalm 139: *"Lord, You have searched me and You know me. You know when I sit and when I rise; You perceive my thoughts from afar. You discern my going out and my lying down; You are familiar with all my ways. Before a word is on my tongue You know it completely, O Lord"* (vv. 1-4).

He did not use His Word as a battering ram to break me down, as I had feared, but rather He used it to shine His light on my misperceptions about how He viewed me. As He unfurled His living Word across my heart, I was awakened to His love for me, my love for Him, and my need for both.

I needed His grace to loosen up my tight grip on my past so I could release it to His loving compassion, and grow from there. He revealed to me that He is big enough to handle what I actually went through, not just my preferred dignified version of it.

When I could no longer ignore the relentless desire to be known by God, I realized that it was never my idea; *it was His.* That made it easier to take the first step in allowing Him to take up residence amidst my stuff. It was as if I invited Him in to a room like you might see on the reality TV show, *Hoarders;* except it wasn't a visible collection of saved junk, it was invisible. He came in and set grace loose right smack in the middle of my history. The shock for me was when I realized He was delighted to be there! Nothing surprised Him. He walked through my shame, fear, abandonment, and abuse without disgust. As a matter of fact, His reaction was far from disgust. This only increased my desire to know Him and be known by Him.

He graced-over my shame and tenderly brought me closer to His accepting heart. I knew that I was fully known and fully accepted. Fully accepted and fully received. Fully received and fully pleasing to God. Amazing grace. I discovered that He wanted to be welcomed into the very center of my being to bring light to what I would prefer to leave in darkness, and to heal what I never thought could be healed. Yes, this longing to be known was a good thing; in fact, it was a God-thing.

One of the most healing aspects of my journey in learning to embrace being known by God is that He never misunderstands me. Having often felt misunderstood as a little girl, it was a really big deal for me to learn that God knows my thoughts and motivations and still likes me. Jesus often blew the minds of His disciples when He would address the unspoken thoughts and intents of their hearts, yet He never stopped loving them. The same is true for us.

Secret Longing for Intimacy with God

The pure movement of grace in our lives is only sustained through a growing intimacy with the Father. As we come to know His ways, we become more adept in cooperating with Him as He chooses to use us as carriers of His grace. As we learn the rhythms of His love, we develop an unforced capacity to be His representatives of grace.

Early on in my walk with the Lord I would listen to Christian friends speak of their intimate relationship with the Lord. Intimacy was a hard word for me to apply to God. It seemed foreign, unrealistic, and even disrespectful. After all, He was God! But then I would hear people speak of deeply personal times with Him, and I was secretly envious. I didn't know if it was possible for me to experience what they spoke of, but if it was, I wanted it. As I came to realize that God accepted me unconditionally while knowing me completely, I found Him irresistible. I felt an increasing hope for intimacy with Him, even though I didn't fully understand what it meant.

I did understand going to God with my needs, after all I was incredibly needy, but I secretly wondered what it would be like to just go to Him; with no agenda, no requests, no whining. His Word was teaching me that He was approachable: *"The Lord is near to all who call upon Him"* (Psalm 145:18 NASB).

In Matthew 26, Mary of Bethany lavished her inheritance, a costly flask of oil, upon Jesus, and she was ridiculed by the disciples who thought it was wasteful. Jesus, however, received her expression of love for Him and chastised those who trivialized her sacrificial gesture. He is blessed when our affection for Him has first place in our hearts.

David had learned to reduce his life's pursuit to one thing: *"I'm asking God for one thing, only one thing: to live with Him in His house my whole life long. I'll contemplate His beauty; I'll study at His feet"* (Psalm 27:4 MSG).

Now I had made my secret longing known. I had voiced it to friends, I had penned it across my journal, and most importantly, I had cried it out to God. I was reclaiming my ability to speak out for the deepest need and desire of my heart with clarity and determination. This is essential to our personal growth and restoration.

I wanted to learn to pursue God shamelessly. I knew that this progressive knowing would only come through a growing intimate relationship with the One Who knows us fully and loves us completely. The more I have come to know and love Him as Lord, Father, Savior, Friend, and Author of my life, the more I recognize Him across every chapter, page, and event. As I see His active involvement in healing, restoring, and transforming my life; I trust Him all the more. As my relationship with Him began to grow, grace had more access to move in my life. I began to recognize grace in action.

Secret Longing to Know my True Identity

Identity issues in my life began when I learned of my mom's hope that I would be born a boy. This issue of identity was a key and I wanted to unlock the truth. In an effort to feel valued, I worked hard to please my parents and significant adults; mostly through achievements such as good grades, housework, childcare, and whatever else was needed. I was astounded to find out that God loves me as His daughter, regardless of what I did or didn't do.

As His child, I learned that I did not need to prove myself to Him. My identity is settled in the mind of God, and my value is not dependent on my performance, nor does the beauty of grace have anything to do with my performance. In fact, as soon as we bring performance on the scene, grace is upstaged. Why? Because when we feel we need to perform to earn God's grace; grace ceases to be grace. If grace is God's unmerited, undeserved gift to us; we redefine it when we try to earn it. To pursue intimacy with the Father, performance must die.

I am His chosen daughter, forgiven completely, and accepted fully. I had no clue how far reaching these truths would go into my confused heart. I felt like He was shaking up this living container of His grace: *me!* The God of the Universe considered me His daughter and I didn't have to do or be anything to receive His love. This was beyond incredible. Something was coming alive in me. My daughter heart was recognizing my Daddy in ways I had never seen Him before. Everything I would read in the Bible about God was telling me how He viewed me. He was carving out my new identity. Over the next several months I would learn that my identity as His beloved daughter meant more than I could have ever dreamed. Below are some Truths God has used to reveal my true identity in Him:

- I am God's child (John 1:12).
- I am Christ's friend (John 15:15).
- I am chosen and appointed by Christ to bear His fruit (John 15:16).
- I am reconciled to God and a minister of reconciliation (2 Corinthians 5:18-19).
- I am God's workmanship, created in Christ to do His work that He planned beforehand that I should do (Ephesians 2:10).
- I have been raised up and seated with Christ in heavenly places (Ephesians 2:6).
- I have been given the mind of Christ (1 Corinthians 2:16).
- I have been bought with a price. I am not my own. I belong to God (1Corinthians 6:19- 20).

When we are confident in our relationship and identity in the Lord, we can stand against the devil and his lies, and we can face rejection, blame, and shame. We won't need to defend ourselves because God is our defense. Jesus needed no defense in the face of His enemies; He knew who He was, and everything He did came as a result of His confident relationship with His Father.

- *"But the Lord has been my defense, and my God the rock of my refuge"* (Psalm 94:22 NKJV).
- *"Be my rock of refuge, a fortress of defense to save me"* (Psalm 31:2 NKJV).

As we discover who God says we are, we are able to walk in the freedom to be who we were intended to be. It is in this discovery that we find our deep need for His grace as well as the reality of His grace.

Grace Like Rain from His Word:

"Meanwhile, the moment we get tired in the waiting, God's Spirit is right alongside helping us along. If we don't know how or what to pray, it doesn't matter. He does our praying in and for us, making prayer out of our wordless sighs, our aching groans. He knows us far better than we know our- selves, knows our pregnant condition, and keeps us present before God. That's why we can be so sure that every detail in our lives of love for God is worked into something good" (Romans 8:26-28 MSG).

"You've always given me breathing room, a place to get away from it all, a lifetime pass to Your safe-house, an open invitation as Your guest. You've always taken me seriously, God, made me welcome among those who know and love You" (Psalm 61:3-5 MSG).

My prayer is that you will be open to recognize your own secret longings. You may discover a desire that was God-planted, just waiting for you to take ownership of it. The most important reason for us to be in touch with the deepest parts of ourselves is so we can recognize His grace at work to transform, heal, and restore our lives. I encourage you to ask God to awaken you to your deepest longings. Allow His enabling grace to help you discover the treasures He has placed within you.

chapter eight

GRACE AND TRUTH

"For the law was given through Moses;
grace and truth *came through Jesus Christ."*
John 1:17 NIV (emphasis mine)

God knew that He had to invade my belief system.
My personal reality had become truth to me and it
needed to be blown to pieces in surrender to God's Truth.
As I began to dig into the Word of God, the scales started
falling from my spiritual eyes and it became increasingly
obvious to me that I had been duped. Not by anyone, but
by life events, and how I had processed those events. God
has used His Word in my life in more ways than I could
possibly catalog within these pages.

Experiences of pain, abuse, abandonment, and betrayal
led to assumptions, which led to introspection, more
assumptions, and those became my belief system. For
example, the pain of hearing that my mom wanted a boy
caused me to believe that I was a disappointment. As a
result, I assumed that my existence was painful to her.
That became my belief. Not being believed when I told
the truth about the chief's abuse, translated into a belief

that I was not credible. Since I didn't know how to give God access to my misperceptions, they became part of my faulty belief system. I accepted them unchallenged, therefore they remained unchanged.

These patterns get us in trouble all the time. Were they facts? As far as I know, to this day, yes. But they were not **God's Truth** for me. Each one of us has bought into ungodly beliefs about ourselves, others, and even God Himself. Something beautiful happens when we surrender our unhealthy beliefs to the transforming redemptive work of God's grace and allow Him to saturate them with His Truth. John 1:14 proclaims that Jesus is *"full of grace and truth."* I do not claim to understand grace, nor do I try. I have experienced the very life of God's grace. Wherever His grace has found me, it has not left me there, but has drawn me closer to Him, thereby changing me. Our transformation comes not only in our grace process, but also as we draw closer to the Lord.

God's grace has destroyed my ego, which is a good thing. God is not looking for sons and daughters with egos. He is looking for surrendered, humble hearts. Where grace travels, it leaves the imprint of God. When He is allowed access to permeate our hearts with His grace, people will see His work as it is displayed through our lives. God receives full credit for His work because grace erases our desire for the spotlight. After all, grace is His gift, and He's the Giver. He deserves complete recognition and honor when His work shows up in our lives. Grace has this amazing capacity to draw us toward the Father's heart while recalibrating ours. I once thought the work of healing my broken heart would take so much energy, but it isn't energy that is extended from us, it is surrender. One requires stamina; the other, release.

When our view of life is clouded by the effects of abuse, hurts, and trauma, we equate our existence with time spent here on earth in our human body. When we allow God's *Grace Like Rain* to pour His healing over our spiritual eyes, time is seen in relation to eternity. In other words, our time here on earth is just a small marker in the grand scheme of our existence. We are not human beings here on earth having a brief *spiritual* experience, but rather we are spiritual beings having a brief *human* experience. Whether you live to be twenty-nine or ninety-nine, it is a brief amount of time when you think of your life in eternal terms.

I love the life-transforming, life-giving Word of God. Second Timothy 3:16 says, *"All Scripture is God-breathed and is useful for teaching, rebuking, correcting and training in righteousness."* It is vital that we not only learn to navigate through the Bible as our guide for living, but also that we recognize it as God's Truth. Truth dispels lies. God's Word is Light. Light dispels darkness. If we want to establish a stronghold of truth in our lives, we need to base our value and worth on the liberating Truth of God's Word. When we allow the Word of God to become our foundation, we find true personal freedom. *"If you hold to My teaching, you are really My disciples. Then you will know the truth, and the truth will set you free"* (John 8:31-32).

In John chapter 8, there is a story of scribes and Pharisees bringing a woman they had caught in adultery before Jesus. The woman is not named in Scripture, and even though she was not known by her name, she was known by her shame. After all, she was brought out into the public to be humiliated for her sin. Who made the scribes and Pharisees the custodians of morality, anyway? There they stood in all their self-righteousness, reminding Jesus that, in the law, Moses commands that the woman should be stoned. Ah, yes. They knew the first part of John 1:7 - *"For the law was given through Moses;"* however, if they hadn't been so busy polishing their stones, they'd have learned the rest – *"but grace and truth came through Jesus Christ."* Then perhaps they wouldn't have had the nerve to ask Jesus their next question: *"What do you say?"*

These were Pharisees; totally not into grace. The accusers were not bringing this woman to Jesus because they saw her as a person in need of Christ's love. They dragged her and dumped her in front of Jesus as their object lesson for the day. Her judgment was not their ultimate goal. The passage says they wanted to trip Jesus up, ultimately so they could accuse Him of something. They were not only ignorant, but arrogant. Jesus responded, saying *"He who is among you, let him throw a stone at her."* They all beat feet, leaving Jesus alone with the woman – the perfect setup for grace in action.

Jesus demonstrated protective grace toward this woman who was about to be tortured. That is what He does for each of us. His truth dispels the accusations and lies of our past, making way for grace to get in our face and show us the bottom line. Jesus said to her: *"I am the light of the world. He who follows Me shall not walk in darkness, but have the light of life."* The Light of the world becomes the Light of our life. Jesus is God's agent of grace. He stepped down from His heavenly throne and demonstrated the heart of the Father's grace toward all of humanity.

Rather than step between the woman and the accusers, Jesus stooped down and wrote in the dirt. Grace gets down in the dirt that surrounds our stuff. Would it be safe to say that *grace gets down and dirty?* He went low to give grace rather than judgment. He went low to give life rather than law. He delivered *Grace Like Rain* over her bondage to bring her into freedom.

We all go through times like the woman in this passage; times that seem unbearable; so horrible we doubt we will recover. When the unthinkable is done against us, or *we do* the unthinkable; we can conclude that we are not worthy of God's love. The truth is that because of grace, we can bounce back, higher and better than we ever dreamed possible.

My mentors in the faith taught me the importance of reading, meditating on, and memorizing Scriptures. It was vital for me to build this foundation to replace my faulty, ungodly belief system. I am blessed that I did not have to do this by myself because I had no clue where to begin. I was a brand new Christian with a messed up life. I thought at the time that God had His work cut out for Him when He saved me. The Truth of His Word taught me that:

- I am deeply loved (1 John 4:9-10).
- I am totally forgiven and fully pleasing to God (Romans 5:1).
- I am accepted by God (Ephesians 1:6).

It looks simple on paper. These were God's powerful Truths crashing up against what I had come to believe about myself: that I was damaged, violated, broken, and not worthy of love. It took patient mentoring, long prayer times, and lots of Kleenex, to cross the bridge into believing that God loved me, forgave me, and accepted me. At first, I wondered when someone was going to lower the boom and finally tell me it was all an illusion. This fear kept one foot in my world of doubt and self-protection.

Life inside my walls had been familiar, safe, predictable, and within the realm of my control. The outside world had always seemed unpredictable and completely beyond my control. I remember wishing I could be invisible as a little girl. On the one hand, I wanted my invisibility to shield me from people and hurt; on the other hand, I ached to be ordinary and to belong. Any time I had tried to blend in with schoolmates or the neighborhood kids, my clumsy attempt would betray that I just wasn't good at being part of the crowd. That only made my case to isolate myself even stronger.

My sense of inner sanctum was fortified by the fact that when I was all closed in, I felt what I thought was peace. It wasn't peace at all, but rather, a false sense of security. The isolation we choose to use as a shield against pain can also become a fortress against intimacy. We can't have it both ways. I believe my protection was initially created to keep me safe; however, isolation actually intensifies our unspoken beliefs regarding shame, blame, and low self-esteem. When a child continually withdraws in isolation, she often concludes that she is one type of person, and everyone else is another. The more we become convinced that we are different, the more it feeds into our tendency to alienate ourselves even further. We isolate in our secret sorrows and keep others from coming close.

Learning to trust Mike was the beginning of my process of taking down my protective walls. I was less than a year old in the Lord and God was answering an unspoken, albeit genuine cry of my heart: to know and be known by God, by Mike, and by others. I also wanted desperately to know myself. *Who was I?* I had always thought of myself in terms of what I did, what happened to me, or what others said was true about me. Those were the safest ways for me to locate my sense of self. I wondered if God had in His bag of tricks some cool way of helping me find my true center. Of course, I would learn that He did; though it wasn't found in a bag of tricks, but in His *Grace Like Rain*.

Now, with God and Mike in my life, I felt I was being redefined – loved, accepted, and valued. Wow! What does a girl do with this? I was beginning to realize that God was using my relationship with Mike to heal the very core of my identity. God asked me if I was willing to allow my protective walls to come down. That was like asking a kid with a badly decayed tooth if she wanted it pulled. No. And yes. But no. My teeter-totter response was in knowing it was going to hurt, but also that it was the best thing for me. If we want to *heal*, we must first *feel*, and then *deal* with our pain.

In order to become pain-free, *pain* usually comes before *free*. Ultimately, I knew that in order to be able to return authentic love to Mike, I had to come out from behind my protective shield. How was I going to be able to take down what had been my only source of protection for so many years? I was uncertain.

We must allow the seeds of information to be transformed into revelation. Reading the Bible doesn't set us free just because we absorb new information. We might grow in understanding, but that still doesn't bring freedom to our lives. Just collecting information about how to be free did not make me free. It showed me that freedom was possible.

God was so gentle in drawing me close to Him. His *Grace Like Rain* soaked me with the words of Psalm 91:2, *"He is my refuge and my fortress, my God, in whom I trust."* I wrote it on index cards, taped it to my bedroom mirror, and kept it on my desk. I was learning that God Himself wanted to be my fortress. The more time I spent with Mike, the easier it was to share with him. Gradually I began to experience a level of comfort and safety that took me by surprise. I realized that the Lord was using Mike to crack my shell.

Grace Like Rain from His Word:

- *"His Word throws a beam of light on our dark path"* (Psalm 119:105 MSG).
- *"His Word is Truth"* (John 17:17 NKJV).

- *"Let them bring me to Your holy mountain, to the place where You dwell"* (Psalm 43:2).
- *"Send forth Your light and Your truth, let them guide me"* (Psalm 43:3).
- *"Show me Your ways, O Lord, teach me Your paths; guide me in Your truth and teach me, for You are God my Savior, and my hope is in You all day long"* (Psalm 25:4-5).
- *"Now God, don't hold out on me, don't hold back Your passion. Your love and truth are all that keeps me together"* (Psalm 40:11 MSG).

I began to discover the *no strings attached* aspect of God's grace. There is no requirement for grace. Our heavenly Father doesn't extend His grace to us conditionally upon our good behavior or right response. He extends His grace as the perfect gift of His love. All we need to do is receive His gift. When we live in grace, we are no longer *driven* by external demands or internal rules, but rather we are *drawn* by God's love for us.

It was amazing grace that moved Jesus from heaven to earth, the cross, the grave, and in resurrection power. It was amazing grace that moved the Father to indwell His children with His Holy Spirit. Grace! Don't you just love Him for it? Are you willing to let God get in the face of your stuff, so He can put a new face on it; *the face of grace?*

chapter nine

THE UNFORCED RHYTHMS OF GRACE

September, 1971. Phone calls. Deliveries. Silver. Fine china. Linens. Cookware. Small appliances. And clocks; lots of clocks! This was all evidence that there was only one more month until I married the love of my life. Mike and I had wanted a simple wedding; however, we felt pressure to include my dad's business associates and friends in the big day. They didn't want anyone left out – except my mom. The wedding plans spiraled out of control, and by that I mean, out of *my* control. My stepmother took over the decision-making department; including the reception, caterer, decorations, and the wedding list comprised of people we hardly knew. I tried my best to brush it off; after all, in just a few weeks I would be off on my honeymoon, and the beginning of a new life. I wanted to put my past behind me and move forward.

We attended the required premarital counseling sessions with the priest who would marry us. I was sure he would figure out that I was a mess and advise Mike not to sign on to a life sentence with damaged goods, but he didn't. He read from a manual, barely looking up as he went through the list of questions. Apparently we passed, and the wedding would proceed as scheduled. I realize now that I was just expecting the hammer to come down with some reason to crush my dream.

The wistful atmosphere of my approaching big day was being invaded by my secret pain. I was getting married, and my mom wouldn't be there. Instead, I was watching my wedding evolve into something completely different than I had hoped. As a little girl, I had drawn countless wedding gowns and sketched my dream family in front of a quaint little house, white picket fence and all. I remember daydreaming of planning my special day with my mom: trips to bridal shops with her to find the perfect dress, picking out the reception site, and long talks about what to expect in my single-to-married transition. As I said, that was my dream, but all that came crashing down in my real world. I felt as if I was sinking without warning into the quicksand of disappointment and disillusionment.

One day when my dad asked why I seemed sad during what should have been the happiest time of my life, I told him I wished my mom was here. His response was clear: I had crossed over into the forbidden zone. Yes, I remembered that he had told us we were not to mention our mother, *but he asked*. My dad interpreted my state-ment as a selfish lack of appreciation for all the work my stepmother was putting into planning my wedding. I was taken aback; certainly it was not my intent to disappoint my dad. I had lowered my wall to tell him how I felt, now I felt bulldozed back into my corner. I decided to keep the peace until we could get through the wedding. In a few weeks I would be out of there and life would be good.

The wedding planning continued and for the most part I remained a spectator. Mike and I did get to choose our flowers, our wedding party and their formalwear. I had found the wedding gown of my dreams in a magazine and a local bridal shop was able to order it. A week before my wedding, the shop called to say the alterations were finished and I could come in to pick up my dress. I was ecstatic. I brought my cousin, one of my bridesmaids, with me.

To my horror, when they had altered the dress, the zipper was now two inches off-center. They had only taken in the dress on the right side! I was devastated. The bridal consultant tried to convince me that it was fine and not noticeable. My cousin insisted otherwise and asked for the store manager. Upon inspection, she apologized for the seamstress's wrongdoing, and advised me that since there was no time to get another dress, I would have to choose one in stock. There was no other dress in the store that even came close to the first one, so they appeased me with store credit and we left.

I called Mike and hysterically tried to explain to him what had happened. He had (and still has) this amazing ability to calm me down. He told me to shop for another dress and he would pay for it. My husband-to-be took care of my dress-distress and purchased my second wedding gown. It wasn't nearly as elegant as the one that was ruined, but it was a thousand times more special because of the love behind it. To me, this was more evidence that God was going to use this man to help heal my heart.

The next week is a blur, undoubtedly because I was plowing full steam ahead through all the final details leading up to the big event. On my wedding day, October 2, 1971, I woke before dawn, impatiently counting the hours until I would be *Mrs. Michael Kriesel*. I had written those words out hundreds of times as I daydreamed of becoming his bride. Determined to get to the church early, I was ready an hour ahead of schedule and rushed everyone through the photo session at our house. My dad and I arrived at the church thirty minutes before time, and I stationed myself to greet the guests as they walked through the door. (I still can't believe I actually did that!)

I don't remember one word from our wedding ceremony. I do recall standing at the altar in the dress Mike bought for me; captured by his wide grin, thinking – *this is the man who is going to make me happy forever.* After our reception, we left to honeymoon in Old Orchard Beach, Maine, and returned to start our married life in a used mobile home. I was beginning my new life with my new husband and my new name. As naïve as it sounds, I thought I had just stepped into my very own fairy tale.

Beginning a life of love and laughter with Mike had landed me fully into my dream. What I soon realized was that not only did we move into our new place, but my emotional baggage moved right in with me, or actually, *with us.* I was about to discover that my heart was still filled with pain from the past. Places of insecurity, fear, abandonment, trust, and shame, started to surface. Mike and I loved each other, yet we both brought our personal history into our marriage; including the good, the bad and the ugly. Marriage doesn't make a person happy. Only God can do that.

I was learning that even though we loved each other, I couldn't expect Mike to heal my heart. I needed to put the pain of my past where it belonged: in God's hands. In spite of what we go through, there is hope in Christ for our wounds to be healed. In Matthew 11:28-30 Jesus said, *"Are you tired? Worn out? Burned out on religion? Come to Me. Get away with Me and you'll recover your life. I'll show you how to take a real rest. Walk with Me and work with Me — watch how I do it. Learn the **unforced rhythms of grace**. I won't lay anything heavy or ill-fitting on you. Keep company with Me and you'll learn to live freely and lightly"* (MSG, emphasis mine).

Without realizing it, God had just enrolled me in the classroom of learning the *unforced rhythms of grace.* I wanted to be healed more than anything, but I had a long road ahead of me and so did my new husband. The passage in Matthew eleven gave me a new view on grace. It taught me that grace has a rhythm, and it's unforced. I discovered that Jesus had already made a way for my recovery; He was going to teach me the ways of grace and wanted me to partner with Him.

The Unforced Rhythms of Grace to Accept God's Love

One of my first steps in overcoming past hurts was to admit that I had a great need to receive the healing power of God's love. I was quick to recite verses about His love. I knew it was His love that had saved me through Jesus' sacrifice on the cross. Now I needed to learn how to remove my layers of protection and allow His love to do its work in me.

Mike loved me to the best of his ability, yet we both kept bumping into my issues. I was crippled by fears, and through no fault of my husband, I had difficulty trusting. I didn't want to be bound by my past, but I didn't know how to break free. I was painfully insecure, and no matter how much he tried, he couldn't keep up with my desperation for affirmation. He was extremely trustworthy, yet I secretly wondered if he would eventually become frustrated with me and leave. I became possessive and suspicious.

Without realizing it, I was looking to my husband to provide for me what I had been unable to provide for myself. I had put an unspoken, unfair demand on Mike to be my source of affirmation and safety, rather than looking to God as my source. This is too great a burden to put on any human being. If we don't find our source of life, love, and peace in the unconditional love of God, we will continually look to people to meet our needs. Where does a bride go to talk about such confusing, shameful issues?

We were never intended to place our security in other people, but rather in God and His Word. No one human being should have the responsibility of making us feel happy or secure. I needed to learn to trust the Lord as my source of peace. This was no overnight venture. I was broken, and Mike couldn't fix me. I missed my mom, I missed my siblings, and I had intimacy issues as a result of the violation of abuse. I loved being Mike's wife, but now realized that I had unconsciously assumed that marriage would fix all my broken parts.

The Unforced Rhythms of Grace for the Great Exchange

I was learning that God wanted His Word to become my foundation, not Mike or any other person. My personal stability was only going to grow in proportion to my willingness to surrender to the Truth of God's Word. I was experiencing amazing truth encounters which called for the greatest exchange of my life. God wanted my life because He gave the life of His Son, Jesus, for me. He wanted me to exchange my views of me for His. This was part of learning the *unforced rhythms of grace*. The rhythm of His grace went something like this – I release; He replaces. I release; He replaces. I could walk to this beat. I needed to learn to say yes to His Truth so His *Grace Like Rain* could renew my mind. Here are some of the rhythms of my exchange with God:

- Jesus was wounded in order for me to be healed.
- Jesus took my sin so I could be in right standing with God.

- Jesus was punished so I could be forgiven.
- Jesus died a death He didn't deserve to give me a life I could never earn.
- Jesus became a curse so that I could be blessed.
- Jesus became poor so I might become rich through His abundant grace.
- Jesus bore my shame so I could release mine.
- Jesus endured rejection so I could be accepted as a daughter of God.

I realized that it had been unrealistic for me to expect my heart to be healed by marrying the man of my dreams. He was not God's *answer* to my life; he was God's *gift* to my life. *God was the answer to my life.* This was sobering, yet promising, because now I had hope that God not only *could* heal my heart, I had hope that He *would*. My heavenly Father was beginning His beautiful divine exchange with me: my facts for His Truth. Every aspect of my healing would flow from who God is, what He has done for me, and what His Word says is true.

Grace for Mental Strongholds

Over time, as we continue to believe what is not true according to the Word of God, we develop mental strongholds. These strongholds contain lies about us, God, His Word, and other people. A stronghold is a point of access, a base of operation that the enemy uses to keep us crippled from our past. Understanding this was vital in learning to identify the strongholds in my mind. My attempts to stop thinking negative unhealthy thoughts failed. Then I had negative unhealthy thoughts about not being able to stop thinking those thoughts. It was a vicious circle.

Strongholds are *strong holds* on our thought life. They include lies against what God has revealed about Himself in His Word. These strongholds give the enemy permission to traffic in our thought life. Where I felt shame, there was an entire fortress of thoughts supporting my reasons for that shame. Where I was feeling damaged, there was a virtual citadel erected to remind me of all the ways I was broken and no good. These strongholds were rigid and unyielding. They were also effective because I believed the lies that were holding me captive.

In John 8:44, Jesus speaks of our enemy as the father of lies: *"There is no truth in him. When he lies, he speaks his native language, for he is a liar and the father of lies."* It was a major awakening to me to learn that my thought life is either under the influence of my heavenly Father, or the father of lies. When we accept the lies of the enemy we remain disabled. We settle for less because it has become our norm.

But God! I am so thankful that He has made a way for our freedom, no matter how hard the enemy has tried to hold us in chains of deception. My first assignment was to allow truth to penetrate the lies. I needed to identify and confront the lies I had believed. We can't conquer what we aren't willing to confront, and we can't confront what we aren't willing to identify. The bottom line is, *if we don't deal, we won't heal.* I knew that I wanted freedom regardless of the cost. My belief system was polluted with untruths. I needed and wanted an overhaul in my thought life.

The Bible tells us to bring *"every thought into captivity to the obedience of Christ"* (2 Corinthians 10:7 NKJV). We overcome faulty thinking by choosing to believe God's Truth. Philippians 4:8 admonishes us to: *"Think about the things that are good and worthy of praise. Think about the things that are true and honorable and right and pure and beautiful and respected"* (NCV).

I had to learn to be proactive. I needed to be aware of my thought patterns and intercept them before they became beliefs. For example, if I was feeling insecure about my husband's love, I would think that he would eventually get tired of putting up with me and leave. I needed to put those thoughts through the Philippians 4:8 filter: *Were my thoughts good? Praiseworthy? True? Honorable? Right? Pure? No!* Then I needed to replace my wrong thinking with what I knew to be true: *My husband loves me. God loves me. I am valuable to both of them.*

I had to replace the lies I had come to believe with the Truth of God's Word. I was God's daughter and He wanted me to begin thinking, acting, and believing like one. This was such an awakening for me.

This part of my restoration was like peeling an onion. After one layer of lies was exposed by God's Truth, it was peeled away and then replaced with truth. This continued as God helped me fortify my belief system with truth instead of self-protection. My heart was being changed, softened, and tenderized by the unchanging, unconditional love of my heavenly Father.

Grace Like Rain from His Word:

"Before you know it, a sense of God's wholeness, everything coming together for good, will come and settle you down. It's wonderful what happens when Christ displaces worry at the center of your life" (Philippians 4:7 MSG).

God wants us to know our identity in Christ, and to base our emotional, mental, and spiritual health on His Truth:

- He will never leave us or forsake us (Hebrews 13:5).
- He has completely forgiven us (Colossians 2:13-14).
- He will supply all of our needs (Philippians 4:19).

- There is no condemnation for those who are in Christ Jesus (Romans 8:1).
- We can do all things through Christ who strengthens us (Philippians 4:13).
- God has not given us a spirit of fear, but of love, power and a sound mind (2 Timothy 1:7).
- The peace of God guards our heart and mind in Christ Jesus (Philippians 4:7).

These verses are vital for renewing our minds. God's Word is not only written across the pages of the Bible, but also on the tablets of our hearts. Our responsibility is to accept and believe what God says about us. He wants us to know that our best days are ahead. He wants to use our lives to show the world the power of His grace. He not only desires for us to spend eternity with Him in heaven, He wants us to live a vibrant, passionate, effective life here on earth.

If you struggle to maintain a healthy thought life, you are not alone. Every one of us has to face our individual battle for the mind. Each one of us lives out of what we have come to believe to be true about ourselves; so when we don't see ourselves the way God sees us, we function from lies we have believed. Jesus accepts us just as we are but loves us too much to leave us that way. He died not only to save us from an eternity in hell, but also to save us from ourselves. He has made a way for us not only to *get* free, but *stay* free and *live* free. When we come to believe what God's Word says about us as His sons and daughters, we can build a solid foundation for victorious living.

"The weapons we fight with are not the weapons of the world. On the contrary, they have divine power to demolish strongholds" (2 Corinthians 10:4).

chapter ten

CARRIERS OF PURPOSE

"For it is God who works in you to will and to act
according to His good purpose."
Philippians 2:13

"And we know that in all things God works
for the good of those
who love Him, who have been called
according to His purpose."
Romans 8:28

T he first year of our marriage was a huge learning curve for both of us. Mike and I were completely in love and excited about our new future, but we didn't really know how to do life together. We knew we both had issues, yet we were determined to move forward as lovers, friends, and partners for life. We both wanted to forge ahead in spite of our limited understanding about what to do after we said, "I do."

As I shared earlier, just ten months after our wedding, Mike's sixteen-year-old sister Becky died suddenly, leaving our family awash in grief. In the following months, as people shared their love for Becky, Mike was deeply touched to learn that his younger sister had lived with such purpose. Still, he kept his desire to know God to himself, and I learned (eventually!) to stop pressuring him to come to church. Christian friends wisely counseled me to let God draw Mike to Himself; my assignment was to grow more in love with both of them. Basically, they were telling me to stop nagging my husband, and let God be God. This proved to be great advice, which I have passed on multiple times to other women throughout the years.

Not only would God draw Mike to Himself, but He would continue to teach me how to take responsibility for my own happiness, my own peace of mind, and ultimately my own healing and restoration. I was learning that the more I grew in my relationship with the Lord, the more I could trust Him to help me come out of my cave of isolation and cooperate with His process of transformation. Sounds good on paper, but it was a painful, heart-wrenching journey as I learned to lay down my pain and allow His healing *Grace Like Rain* to saturate my life. I wanted to be a godly wife, and eventually a godly mom and nana, and I knew that if I did not allow God to heal my heart, I would continually carry all my hurt into my relationships with them.

I knew God was calling me to embark on the journey of a lifetime, and I knew it would require me to surrender my wounded heart to Him. Only His perfect heart could touch my broken one. He was looking for just four words from me: "Yes, Lord, I surrender." Little words with huge implications. I was in. No going back. I wanted Him to take over my life and transform me into what He always had in mind for me to be. He was going to help me see that I had a destiny and purpose.

During the tumultuous times in my early years, I had never thought of purpose; at least not where my life was concerned. Survival, yes. Purpose, no. When we are in survival mode, we have tunnel vision. We see what we need to see to make it to the next place. We don't see the possibilities that lie ahead. A woman victimized by childhood sexual abuse has built such a strong system of protection around her heart that she cannot focus on purpose. Rather, she is consumed with ensuring that her fortress remains strong. *She* is not strong; her *fortress* is strong. Impenetrable. That is survival. Abuse victims might indeed seem purposeful as they forge through life with a stoic determined focus; however, their focus remains inward.

Only God can show us our true purpose. He causes it to emerge in His timing like a sunrise, slowly bringing everything into the light, and giving understanding to confusing collections of past and present experiences. He may not reveal why certain things happened, but He does show us how those experiences are valuable to His overall plan for us.

I knew that to live with purpose was far more than to merely function. It was going to take the miracle of Christ working *in* my life, to cause me to be a carrier of His purpose. Honestly, I didn't understand what it all meant, but I wanted to discover that my life had value to God. He was gracing over my sense of inadequacy and igniting a secret hope to find His Kingdom purpose for my life.

Whether we recognize it or not, there is a deep desire inside each of us to live a life of purpose. You and I were created *on* purpose, and *for* purpose. He has built purpose into our spiritual makeup. Purpose is a part of our divine calling. The God of all purpose built purpose into His plan for us, and it is meant to be more than an elusive concept. God was intentional when He created each of us. To wonder if past hurts and wounds can keep us from a life of purpose is to question the sovereignty of God. *What*

*God did not **choose** for us, He will **use** for us.* No matter what we have been through, He meets us where we are and applies grace. Once our lives are *grace-applied*, they are *purpose-supplied*.

When God said, *"Turn to Me and be saved, all the ends of the earth; for I am God, and there is no other"* (Isaiah 45:22), He was declaring that He is in charge. He is God and His purposes stand. The first and highest purpose for each of us is to live a life that reflects the glory of God. We do this through a passionate intimate relationship with Him, through which He reveals more and more of Himself to us. I want to live a life of purpose. It is up to me to grow in intimacy with God and His Word so I can continually discover and rediscover that purpose.

"No eye has seen, no ear has heard, no mind has conceived what God has prepared for those who love Him" (1 Corinthians 2:9). I desperately want to dive into those things He has prepared for me. We were each created with one main purpose: to bring glory to God. Engrained in His main purpose is a personal, tailor-made, one-of-a-kind purpose, placed by God in each of His children. For me, this truth is both humbling and incredible. Knowing my own heart, I wonder how this can be possible, but God has His mind made up where we are concerned. He knows what we have been through, and He knows exactly how He wants our lives to unfold. He knows the end from the beginning, and He is determined to pursue us because He knows that our greatest joys will come as we walk in His plan for our lives. When we understand that God is determined where we are concerned, and we get determined where He is concerned; our lives will be radically transformed. There will be no stopping us from fulfilling the God-ordained destiny He has in mind for us.

As we realize that God not only wants to display His work in our lives, but He also wants to reveal the truth about who He is; we become more intentional in cooperating with His purposes. Our past does not define us. God does. The mystery of grace is that it is never late and always on time. We are God's creation, and He does not view us through the distortion of life events. He views us through love. He views us through grace. When we view our lives through His perspective, we discover our purpose. Our heavenly Father sends His *Grace Like Rain* to liberate us to walk in our God-ordained purpose.

"My determined purpose is that I may know Him [that I may progressively become more deeply and intimately acquainted with Him]" (Philippians 3:10 AMP). Paul says his determined purpose is to have a progressive, deep, and intimate relationship with the Lord. I had read about Paul's life and knew that he wasn't raised as a believer. In fact, he was a murderous terrorist and a hater of Christ and His followers.

Paul knew what it felt like to be misunderstood, mistreated, forgotten, abused, shipwrecked, imprisoned, starving, and left for dead. The Bible describes his miraculous face-to-face encounter with Jesus Christ, and how that grace encounter took Paul from darkness into the glorious light of God's forgiveness. If God could instill true purpose in Paul's heart, I knew He could make that same grace deposit in mine. The magnetic pull on Paul's heart to know the grace-Giver intimately, came as a result of his immense gratitude for that grace.

I am inspired as I read about people in Scripture, like Paul, who faced life-threatening challenges and how God used their circumstances as opportunities to take them deeper into their purpose and destiny. It was through those tests and trials that they learned complete dependence on God and found themselves in the grip of His grace; the grip that never lets go.

"All praise to the God and Father of our Master, Jesus the Messiah! Father of all mercy! God of all healing counsel! He comes alongside us when we go through hard times, and before you know it, He brings us alongside someone else who is going through hard times so that we can be there for that person just as God was there for us" (2 Corinthians 1:3-4 MSG).

I have come to love the word *purpose*. I can live with pain. I can live with trauma. I can live without many things, but I cannot live without purpose. We can view life events differently as we understand that God can rain His grace over them and saturate them with purpose. It is vital that we discover that God has a purpose for our lives, and in preparing us for that purpose, He paints our history with His healing grace.

Once a place of pain is saturated with God's grace, it becomes a place of refreshing for others; a pool of living water we can offer to others. Why? Because when our hurts are washed by His grace, our hearts are positioned to lead others to the God of grace. Knowing we have purpose, and knowing that our grace-saturated places have purpose, brings new meaning to every aspect of life.

Paul tells us that God comes alongside us as our Comforter during our difficulty and ministers to us, which in turn positions us for purpose in the lives of others. I'm sure you have known people who have gone through tragedy such as the loss of a child or a battle with cancer. These people understand better than anyone how to comfort others facing the same dark tunnel. They have experienced the same emotions, fears, and deep grief their friend is facing, and can comfort them as they have been comforted.

This is exactly what God has done in my life. In healing my heart from the affects of abuse and abandonment,

God has equipped me to comfort those He sends my way with the same grace He used to comfort me. We travel with the grace that has been extended to us, and then we invite others into their own grace experience.

The core purpose of life is simple: to know and love God. Out of that simplicity, every good thing we are and every good thing we do will flow. As a result of sexual abuse, I had lived my life with one hand trying to hold everything together, and the other making sure only safe people entered my life. Both are exhausting and impossible. God was showing me that He wants me to be all about one thing: Him. He is not the most important thing in life. *He is the **only** thing.* He is our life. I wanted to become a radical lover of Jesus.

Paul says, *"When Christ (your real life, remember) shows up again on this earth, you'll show up, too"* (Colossians 3:4 MSG). ***Christ is our real life!*** God birthed an excitement in me and a desire to go for it – to trust Him to show me what it means for Christ to *be* my life. It was beyond my understanding as a new believer, but somehow I knew this Kingdom Truth was a key to my healing and restoration.

The world is not looking for perfect people who have it all together. The world is looking for ordinary people whose pain, sin, and trauma have collided with the grace of God, resulting in hope, joy, peace, and purpose. This gives others hope that He can do the same for them. There are times when grace is rained on our everyday, ordinary path, and our life seems to take shape. We not only find purpose, but we become people of purpose. He braids the strands of our history, destiny, and purpose together; pours His grace over it, and then delightfully presents it to us as a gift.

God desires each of us to be purposeful, authentic carriers of His grace and redemption toward mankind.

Not just people who can quote verses on grace or explain grace, but those who have allowed His *Grace Like Rain* to drench our hearts, and cleanse our sin and shame. In order to be a carrier of purpose, we must determine in our hearts and minds that He is trustworthy to take us back to His original intent for us, and heal anything and everything that has kept us from that intent. That is when we can carry the true purpose of the King and His Kingdom in our lives.

Grace Like Rain from His Word:

"But the Lord has become my fortress, and my God the rock in whom I take refuge" (Psalm 94:22).

"Your very lives are a letter that anyone can read by just looking at you. Christ Himself wrote it — not with ink, but with God's living Spirit; not chiseled into stone, but carved into human lives — and we publish it" (2 Corinthians 3:2-3 MSG).

chapter eleven

GRACE-INFUSED FORGIVENESS

O ur first anniversary presented us with a two-fold reason to celebrate; not only our first year of marriage, but also the big news that we would soon become parents. Mike and I knew early in our relationship that we wanted to have children and we were ecstatic. I couldn't wait to be a mom and I knew my husband would be an amazing dad. We spent the next several days telling our good news to anyone who would listen. We started wandering through the infant clothing and furniture departments. I bought fabric and patterns to begin sewing what I thought were the cutest maternity tops ever. I look back at photos and am aghast that I actually wore them in public.

The first three months of my pregnancy brought the expected morning sickness, but it also unexpectedly surfaced residual emotions concerning my relationship with my own mom. I have no doubt now that the timing was perfectly orchestrated by God. He had been saturating my daughter heart with His *Grace Like Rain,* bringing healing into every place of hurt. He had been teaching me to tear down strongholds in my mind; He had been helping me face His truth about my identity in Christ, and now He was awakening my heart to His love and acceptance for me as His child. I had been reading, believing, and memorizing verses in the Bible about how my heavenly Father viewed me. I had not anticipated feeling a sense of longing for my mom.

As a little girl, all my fairy tale dreams of my role as a wife and mother included my parents' involvement in my children's lives. In that world, I had imagined play dates, sleepovers, and happy times for my kids with their grandparents. When I would think of the type of grandparents I would want my baby to be around, I would borrow my dream from what I saw in my friends' families. I had seen some examples of kind, fun, nurturing grandparents and decided that's what I wanted for my kids. I hadn't given up on dreaming for my mom to know and love my children, so I scraped up every possible good memory of my mom to keep that dream alive. Still, I faced the stinging reality that my mom was out of my life, and my baby may never know my mother unless something changed.

Without my realizing it, as God was pouring out His love on me as His daughter, His *Grace Like Rain* was melting the icy walls of protection I had placed around my heart as my mother's daughter. I wasn't thrilled at how vulnerable I was feeling. After all, I had taken charge of my inner courts to decide who got entry and who didn't. My protective walls weren't doing their job keeping me from feeling tender toward my mom. God was taking down the barrier, and though it was frightening on one level, it was freeing on another. It was frightening because it was unfamiliar. It was freeing because I knew that if I was missing my mother, God must be in the picture. He is attentive to our secret, unspoken desires even before we are aware that we want Him involved. God was softening my heart so He could heal it and He was revealing His love for me.

As my tummy grew, so did my longing for my mom. Even though I had bought into all the reasons my dad had severed our relationship with her; that logic wasn't quite working for me anymore. Now I was feeling sentimental, mushy, and even weepy where my mom was concerned. I tried brushing it off, blaming my sensitivity on the mood swings of a pregnant woman. Deep down I knew God was awakening something inside me that had goodness attached to it.

Over the next several months, God used the desperation in my heart to draw me close to Him through His Word. I began to cry out to the Lord using the Psalms because I had no idea where to start on my own. I am thankful for the honesty and transparency of the psalmists, and to this day I continue to borrow from their words when I can't seem to find my own.

"Everything's falling apart on me, God; put me together again with Your Word" (Psalm 119:107 MSG). I honestly felt as if everything was falling apart inside of me. When old belief systems are invaded by God's grace, it can seem unsettling until we get our footing in His Word.

"I cry out to God Most High, to God, who fulfills His purpose for me" (Psalm 57:2). I wondered what God's purpose for me was concerning my mother. I asked Him to show me. I needed understanding. My mom was gone and my heart ached for her. Could God possibly fix this? *"May my cry come before You, O Lord; give me understanding according to Your Word"* (Psalm 119:169). Sometimes I felt like God was off on another assignment. In these times when He seemed distant and aloof, it increased my desperation for Him. I now know that God was using this season to draw me close to Him through His Word. His Word is true, and though He may seem far away, He is close. *"Hear my prayer, O Lord; let my cry for help come to You. Do not hide Your face from me when I*

am in distress. Turn Your ear to me; when I call, answer me quickly" (Psalm 102:1-2).

"There's nothing like the written Word of God for showing you the way. . . Through the Word we are put together and shaped up for the tasks God has for us" (2 Timothy 3:15,17 MSG). I knew God had an assignment in His lesson plan for me. I also knew the assignment involved restoration in my relationship with my mother. I was learning that when God calls us to do something, He also equips us for that call. I didn't feel equipped yet, but I knew I was being prepared to take steps toward my mom.

"God can't break His Word. And because His Word cannot change, the promise is likewise unchangeable" (Hebrews 6:18 MSG). Sometimes we take what we have learned to be true about our earthly parents and we unknowingly assign it to God's character. When we have felt abandoned by our earthly parents, we may doubt God's faithful presence. If our experience has been betrayal, we may have trouble trusting God. As we grow in Him, we come to know and trust Him as a Father who keeps His Word, and whose promises never change.

"In simple humility, let our gardener, God, landscape you with the Word, making a salvation-garden of your life" (James 1:21 MSG). When I picture this verse in my mind, I see myself letting go and giving God the freedom to do what He wants in landscaping my heart with His Word. As a young girl, I watched a landscaper transform my grandfather's property into something right out of a lawn and garden magazine. He relocated rocks that were already there, positioning them around newly planted flower gardens and shrubs. He removed anything that did not fit his overall picture for the new landscape and made room for beautiful new foliage.

God does this with us. He takes those things that we used to trip over and repositions them to display His grace-garden through our lives. He uses our stumbling blocks as stepping stones to show off His transforming redemptive work in us. I love this about Him!

I knew He was a God of reconciliation; after all, He had sent His Son to reconcile the world back to Him. But I also knew it was personal. I had heard testimonies from other Christians about how God had healed hurts and restored relationships, and it had all come through one river of grace: forgiveness. I knew I wanted God to restore my relationship with my mother. I also knew that I needed to forgive her on many levels: disappointment that I was a girl; disbelief concerning the chief's abuse; continuing to take me to his house; leaving my dad for another man, and taking the three little kids with her. I knew I would have to face my feelings of abandonment, betrayal, loss, grief.

I needed God's grace to move me beyond needing answers, to the One who *is* the answer. I had begun to know Him as a loving Father, and now He was calling me to trust that He is the One who ultimately can heal my relationship with my mom and show me how to move forward. Searching for the elusive why, how, or what if, would only serve to distract me. Every time I had tried to answer my own questions about my mom and my relationship with her, I only dug a deeper hole and became even more stuck.

Jesus said in John 14:6, *"I am the way and the truth and the life."* He wasn't just offering me a way; He IS the way. He wasn't just offering me truth; He IS truth. He wasn't just offering me life; He IS life. In John 8:31-32, Jesus said, *"If you hold to My teaching, you are really My disciples. Then you will know the truth, and the truth will set you free."* God was showing me that I could be free, and freedom is found in the Person of Jesus Christ and in the Truth of His Word.

I had long talks with God about my desire to reconnect with my mom. I also had long talks with Mike, sharing with him what God was showing me. Mike was protective, but encouraged me to pursue my relationship with my mother, assuring me of his support. I found out where she had moved and got her mailing address so I could write her a letter. I had not heard from her since she had left four years earlier. I longed for the results of forgiveness, but I was apprehensive about the process. The process scared me.

When we experience the forgiving power of God's grace in our lives, we are equipped to be forgivers. I had experienced His forgiveness in my life. It was a miracle of love to me in knowing that God sent His Son to die for me. I wanted Him to show me how to forgive my mom and help me rebuild my relationship with her. I was sure that the idea of reconciliation with my mom came straight from God's heart.

I do not expect forgiveness to bubble up in you just because you are reading this chapter. When I have had the opportunity to share my forgiveness journey publicly, those who have experienced violation or abuse have expressed their reluctance to forgive, and their difficulty with the suggestion that their abuser should be forgiven. This is an understandable reaction. If we want freedom from the pain of our past, it is vital that we forgive those who have hurt us.

The gift of forgiveness we extend to another person is really a gift we give to ourselves. Forgiveness not only lets the offender off the hook, but most importantly, it allows us to be set free from the endless cycle of pain, anger, shame, and everything else that has kept us imprisoned. As long as I held on to what my mother did to me, I would remain trapped in a dance of misery with her.

I started my letter to my mom with all the reasons I was extending forgiveness to her, and then I stopped abruptly. I knew something was wrong, so I laid my head on my paper and got quiet before the Lord. I asked Him to speak to me. And He did. He gently showed me that I was justifying all my reasons my mother needed forgiveness from me. I was in blame mode. Oh, I forgot to mention that whenever I felt like God didn't understand me regarding my feelings of shame, rejection, and betrayal; I would usually shift into blame mode, victim mode, or pity-me-please mode. God does not play games with His children, nor does He appreciate it when we try to play games with Him. Basically, when I tried to play the game – any game – He wouldn't play. Eventually, I had to come around and get real. *That's* what He likes. God was so patient with me.

When I got real with God and got real with myself, He began to show me that I had an offended, unforgiving heart. I was horrified to think that my heart was displeasing to the God I loved so much. An unforgiving heart will drag us down and it becomes a dumping station for the enemy to unload more lies, logic, and junk to distract us from the true destiny God has for us. My offended heart was an offense to God.

When we refuse to forgive, it is evidence that we are proud. James 4:6 says, *"God resists the proud, but gives grace to the humble."* When, in pride, we refuse to forgive, we are cultivating the environment for bitterness to thrive. If we refuse to forgive, we will never move beyond the pain in our lives. I was harboring offense in my heart and the only cure for offense is forgiveness. Forgiveness is not offered to us as an option; it is a command.

Now I had to make a crucial decision: did I want my heart to stay filled with anger, disappointment and hurt, or would I pursue His heart and allow Him to change mine? Ephesians 4:30-32 is clear: *"Don't grieve God. Don't break His heart. His Holy Spirit, moving and breathing in you, is the most intimate part of your life, making you fit for Himself. Don't take such a gift for granted. Be gentle with one another, sensitive. Forgive one another as quickly and thoroughly as God in Christ forgave you"* (MSG). I knew I didn't want to grieve God or break His heart. I knew that I had received amazing forgiveness from God, and I also knew He was asking me to forgive my mom.

No matter what you have gone through, I want to encourage you to become a forgiver. The only way to move past the hurts of life and move forward is through forgiveness. It is impossible to forgive without an infusion of God's grace into our hearts. We may not feel like forgiving, but God gives grace that goes beyond our feeling. Since God is a forgiver, all we need to do is decide to line ourselves up with Him. It is within our spiritual DNA to be forgivers. This did not come quickly to me, nor did it come easily. However, once I made the decision to forgive, I knew I had signed on and there was no turning back.

Over the next several months, I dedicated myself to study true, biblical forgiveness. Forgiveness is God's greatest expression of love, grace, and mercy toward us in sending His Son as a ransom for our sins. It was clearly a contrast to what I had grown up with. In my family, when we had to apologize to one another as kids, we would usually grumble out the token, "I'm sorry," to appease our parents. The other child was then expected to say, "I forgive you," and apparently the verbal exchange was sufficient. God's version of forgiveness has nothing to do with the word of apology. He looks for a heart change that supersedes verbiage.

When trust issues cause a breakdown in our relationships, if we are not carriers of grace-infused forgiveness, we become independent. If we cannot rely on others because they have betrayed our trust, and we do not incorporate forgiveness into the equation; we push God aside and rely only on ourselves. Do the math: betrayal minus forgiveness equals independence. Independence minus God's grace equals hardness of heart.

God pinpointed so many areas where my logic was tripping me up. It is hard to forgive after trust has been shattered. He was going to take me beyond what I had believed about forgiveness to reveal His Truth. We often settle for reluctant forgiveness; offering it because it's the right thing to do, but our heart has not changed. I learned that God doesn't settle for second-rate forgiveness, neither does He allow us to give forgiveness in certain areas while holding it back in others. God did not want me to forgive my mom in some areas and continue to hold her hostage in others. God was looking for the real deal. I could learn true forgiveness now, through my relationship with my mother, or I could tiptoe around my pain and give it reluctantly or with restriction. I realized that these two lesser impersonations of forgiveness allowed me to maintain some semblance of control. I wanted to be able to protect myself from future hurt, so I was hoping to offer just enough forgiveness to please God, while not completely letting my mom off the hook.

I went into victim mode before God. I maintained that I had been hurt by my mom and yes, I wanted her back in my life, but not at the expense of becoming vulnerable to more pain, betrayal, abandonment or rejection. I think I may have been trying to cut a deal with God. He went silent on me. I hate it when He does that. I had to decide whether to move forward and pursue this relationship or to keep my mom at arm's length and protect myself from further hurt.

I cried out with the psalmist, *"God, don't shut me out; don't give me the silent treatment, O God"* (Psalm 83:1

MSG). In my personal relationship with the Lord, when I slip into spiritual temper tantrums, or go off on Him with my tirade of logic in my meager attempt to change His mind, He simply goes silent. It works with me. It settles me down. It centers me. Thankfully, I eventually come around.

His assignment for me was clearly that He wanted me to learn *grace-infused forgiveness*. When it is *grace-infused*, it is complete. No holding back, no conditions, no terms of agreement. Eventually, I came to terms with the all-inclusive aspect of God's grace. After all, He wasn't selective when He forgave me. He hadn't said, "I forgive you for some sins, but not all." That's when it hit me that He hadn't just forgiven my sins, He had forgiven *me.* Christ's sacrifice on the cross wasn't just for my sins, it was for *me.* He had redeemed *me* – everything about me – past, present, and future. I was His child, and I was grace-washed, and now, grace-infused.

Throughout this process, I came to know God as the most patient and compassionate Teacher I could have imagined. I was a student under the One who had invented forgiveness. It's one thing to have a teacher who knows their subject matter. It's another thing entirely to have a Teacher who IS the subject matter. God is love, and He teaches us to walk in that love. Forgiveness is a direct outflow of His love, and **we are not only called to forgive, but to *become* forgivers.** This, my friend, is the key to discovering the freedom of forgiveness.

He gently spoke and told me that I was not to write a letter forgiving my mom. Rather, I was to write a letter asking my mom to forgive me. *What?* At first I didn't understand. I was confused. *All these months in the school of forgiveness and He wants me to ask for forgiveness? Had I missed a class?* It seemed as if God had turned the table on me, and it was a bit unsettling. There it was again, my logic; my need to get it before I could do it. I finally decided once again, that I could trust God. I knew He loved my mom more than I did, and I knew He wanted our relationship reconciled more than I did. This was my opportunity to hold on to Philippians 1:6, *"God began doing a good work in you, and I am sure He will continue it until it is finished"* (NCV). I decided to go for it, and as I put my pen back to the paper, I watched the ink flow out as *Grace Like Rain* wrote through me. My letter went like this:

Dear Mom,
I know it has been a long time since we have been in touch. Please forgive me for not writing sooner. Forgive me for not trying to reach you after you moved to Colorado. Mike and I got married last year and now we are expecting our first baby. I can't imagine having my baby without you in my life. I miss you. I want you to be a part of my life, and I want to be a part of yours if you would like. I love you and hope we can have a fresh start.
Your daughter, Diana

I was not prepared for my own reaction to writing that letter. First of all, as the words came out, so did a flood of tears. I knew the heart of God was pouring *Grace Like Rain* through the ink onto my paper. He knew what was in my heart better than I did. I was slowly getting in touch with the 'mom void' but God was also revealing something deeper. Buried beneath my hurt, anger, and disappointment toward my mom, was an erupting volcano of love!

It had been easier to live with disappointment, anger and hurt than it was to be in touch with the depth of my love for my mom. Hurt, anger, and disappointment put up walls; love lays walls down flat. Hurt resists; while love invites. Hurt folds its arms; love opens them wide. Hurt says no; love says yes. It felt safe to live within the walls because they had become my self-built defense to help me cope with life. *After all, I had learned to live without her, hadn't I?* Once I got in touch with the love I had in my heart for my mom, I couldn't hold back the tears and what they represented. My letter asking my mom to forgive me was as much for me as it was for her. God leaked those words out of my pen and out of my heart.

It may not make sense to you that my letter was all about asking for forgiveness, rather than forgiving. I didn't totally understand it either. But I did know that it was the right thing to do. Note to self: when it comes to understanding the ways of God, leave logic at home. God's ways are higher than our ways; His ways go beyond our understanding, and His ways carry grace. As a daughter of God, I knew that I had been forgiven, and part of His grace on my life was that I was called to be a forgiver. Forgiveness is part of our inheritance as His children.

God was my Teacher in *Kingdom Forgiveness 101.* I was enrolled in class, and my test was to write the letter to my mom as *God wanted it written.* He knows what He wants delivered to the heart of the person with whom we're reconciling. We may think we have it all figured out, but this is a place we need to depend on Him and push past our logic and limited understanding. I read the letter three times, prayed over it, sealed it in an envelope and sent it off on its grace journey.

I was sure that everything would be okay. My mom would receive my letter, forgive me, and we would be on our way to a fresh new relationship. I anxiously watched for the mailman every day after that. I had mixed feelings. I couldn't wait to hear from her, and yet I was afraid of her reaction. Weeks went by, then months. Almost three months after I wrote that first letter, I got her response in the mail. I tore the envelope open, read my mom's note, and crumbled to the floor. I was brokenhearted.

Diana,
I was very hurt that you did not invite me to your wedding.
I am still your mother, and I should have at least had the
choice whether to go or not.
Mom

Wait! What? That's it? I couldn't believe what I had just read. I held her letter in my hands for several minutes, reading it over and over again. I was in shock and disbelief. *What was I to do? Where do I go from here?* Almost before I recognized it, blame stood up in self-righteous rebuttal. I would write back and tell her "It wasn't my fault you weren't at my wedding; you're the one who walked out on us! After you were gone, dad wouldn't let us contact you!" Then I stopped in my tracks. These thoughts felt horribly wrong. I had taken on the attitude of a defense attorney ready to battle the prosecution. No one was on trial here.

Now I was overwhelmed. My mind was inundated with memories of the ways my mother had ridiculed, abandoned, and hurt me, yet my heart was longing to have her back in my life as well as in the life of my baby. Memories, thoughts, and feelings were all around me, interlocked like a never-ending chain. And then there was my limited experience and understanding of God's version of forgiveness. I was overwhelmed, confused, and exhausted. I had to decide whether to move forward and pursue my relationship with my mom, or keep her at arm's length and protect myself from further hurt.

It felt like my hope for a relationship with my mom was slipping away, and my heart felt like it was being broken into a thousand pieces. Experiencing disappointment does not necessarily reveal a lack of trust. It reveals *disappointment* and God doesn't want us to hide it from Him. He began to show me that I could trust Him even though I was immersed in disappointment. Sometimes I think we assume that in order to trust God, we need to get over whatever we are feeling. This is not true. God wants us to come to Him in our disappointment. He is there, right in the midst of it, inviting us to find our refuge in Him.

My strength to stand in the face of my emotions seemed to collapse. I doubt we can truly know what it means for God to be the strength of our heart until we come to the end of our own strength. Psalm 73:26 says, *"My flesh and my heart may fail, but God is the strength of my heart and my portion forever."*

I felt as if I was at a crossroad; much like the one in *The Wizard of Oz* when Dorothy was skipping down the yellow brick road and suddenly stopped in front of the scarecrow, not knowing whether to go left or right. He first pointed one way, then the other, and then both. I could go left, and retreat back into denial and just try to forget the whole issue with my mom. Or I could go the other way, *the right way*, and surrender my forgiveness process to the Lord. After all, He came up with the whole concept in the first place. I knew that the right thing to do was to let God lead me down what looked like a long, winding path toward my mom's heart. When I said yes to Him, I opened myself up to His grace for my process.

God had allowed things to unfold so that I would know what was in my own heart. Sometimes we resent the circumstances that God wants to use in our lives to develop us. Those things we consider to be roadblocks are actually placed there to slow us down so God can introduce us to the stuff inside us that is holding us back.

My emotional upheaval was a huge reality check. Even though I had begun to walk in the Father's love for me, my experience was still shallow. I was only allowing God's *Grace Like Rain* to flood me up to my ankles. I needed a bigger puddle. A pool. An ocean. I needed to be saturated with forgiving grace so I could be overwhelmed by it and extend it freely as God had done toward me.

Now the question I faced was: *Did I want to pursue my mission, my mother's mission, or did I want to pursue God's mission?* I had to decide whether I was going to respond to her letter in a bitter tirade or was I going to respond to God. I felt shame, grief, and sorrow for having had these nasty feelings. "Lord, forgive me! Here I am, praying that You will restore my relationship with my mom, and I get all angry and defensive when she responds to my letter."

Yes, it was easy to blame my mom and my dad. There were justifiable reasons to go there, but that was then and this was now. I was working on my past and giving God access to my heart. I chose that day to lay it all down and decided not to play the blame card. I had to ask myself two important questions: *How badly did I want this relationship restored? Was I willing to surrender my mom's unexpected response over to the Lord?* I decided then and there that I was in this for the long haul. I had nothing to lose. I had already lost my mother. If I hung in there, it had to get better.

The decision to receive my mom's response without allowing it to push me backwards was a turning point for me. My breakthrough with my mother came as I opened my heart to God's love for her, and opened my heart to her need for His love. God used His grace to allow me to bridge the two. I had a sense of peace. Peace is evidence of a forgiving heart. Forgiveness removes those things that have been preventing us from seeing the truth about

God and the truth about ourselves. It is then that we are able to see the person we are forgiving with God's eyes.

Over the next few weeks, I prayed Scripture and asked God to give me His perspective and His heart for my mom. I borrowed hope from Jeremiah's words: *"But there's one other thing I remember, and remembering, I keep a grip on hope: God's loyal love couldn't have run out, His merciful love couldn't have dried up. They're created new every morning. How great is Your faithfulness!"* (Lamentations 3:21-23 MSG). I asked God to lift me above my own pain to receive His strength when I had none of my own. I asked Him to teach me to respond to Him in faith.

I began to feel stronger. I knew that God would be pleased if I kept my heart pure and did not respond back with retaliation, anger, blame, or defensiveness. I asked God how to respond, and wrote back:

Dear Mom,
Thank you for writing back. I am sorry that you missed my wedding. I was sad too. I hope we can start fresh and try to build our relationship.
Love, Diana

My mom's letter was a grace-given opportunity for me to learn to respond with *grace-infused forgiveness.* As difficult as it was, and as deep as my pain was, I felt a sense of peace in responding God's way rather than mine. It was an exchange: my hurt heart for His love and grace. I discovered that the person who gains the most from forgiveness is not the one to whom the forgiveness is extended, but rather, it is the one who extends grace-infused forgiveness. I still didn't know whether or not my relationship with my mom would be reconciled, but I did know my part: to be like Christ meant I needed to become a forgiver.

Too often, people think that two people must be involved in forgiveness. Though that is true of reconciliation, it is not true of forgiveness. I had forgiven my mom. I was sure of it. Whether we would be reconciled was yet to be seen. It would take two hearts, willing to go the distance together, giving and receiving grace-infused forgiveness. I prayed.

The next letter I received from my mom was generic, but not inflammatory. There were many letters back and forth between us over the next several months. Sometimes I would read them with little hope for our relationship to be healed. I had to lean into my heavenly Father, and trust Him with the heart of my natural mother. It wasn't easy, and though it seemed to take forever, I know God used the waiting period to purify my heart in preparation for what was ahead.

In the meantime, while I was waiting and hoping for a healing with my mother, God turned to an entirely different page in His forgiveness manual. He showed me that I needed to forgive the chief. I hadn't even been thinking about the chief. I didn't know where he lived, or if he was still alive. God ministered to my heart and showed me that He loved the chief. In fact, He loved the chief as much as He loved me. He had loved us both so much that He sent His Son to die for us.

I bristled at the thought of God referring to the chief and me in the same sentence. I never wanted to be in the same room with him again, much less have my heavenly Father refer to us in the same sentence. I think I had this sense of justice running through my veins. If I forgave, where would the justice be? In my heart, I knew that I had to give it up. Forgiveness overrides our need to take justice into our own hands. God never writes people off, and neither can we.

Have you ever been in a quiet prayerful time of communication with God and hear Him say something that sends you off on a tangent? In my mind, I was ranting and raving about all that the chief had done. After I stepped sheepishly down off my soapbox, I was struck by deafening silence. God was there. He was quiet. I knew it was my turn. I realized that I had become enraged over Jesus dying for the man who had violated me as a little girl. I wanted to crawl under the couch. (I forgot to tell you that my favorite place to spend lingering times with God is on my living room floor. So while you are picturing me wallow in my shame over having ranted on God, picture me there.) Not a pretty sight: beached whale pregnant woman laying on her back on the living room floor feeling totally horrified that she had just challenged the love of God.

When it seems as if God has stopped talking to me, I ask Him to show me what is in my heart. He always answers that prayer. This time He showed me my limited view of salvation. I had personalized His gift of salvation. It is personal, but it is not exclusive. God's grace is inclusive, demonstrated by John 3:16, *"For God so loved the **world** that He gave His one and only Son, that **whoever** believes in Him shall not perish but have eternal life"* (emphasis mine). I knew that if I chose not to forgive the chief, it would hurt me more than it would hurt him. I knew my unforgiveness would imprison me. Unforgiveness is toxic; it poisons the thinking and pollutes the heart.

It wasn't all about Diana going to heaven. *God so loved the **world**.* In His love for the world, He made provision for **whoever** *believed* to receive eternal life. I was a *whoever*, Mike was a *whoever*, my baby was a *whoever*, my mom was *whoever*, and the chief was a *whoever*. Yes, God loves the chief, and God sent Jesus to die for him. I wrapped my hands around my baby bump and hugged us. I began to weep with the realization of how broad God's love is for mankind. My focus had been so narrow, and now God was exploding it. I believe this is the moment when He showed me the power and freedom of forgiveness.

I placed the chief and all he had done to me before the Lord, and I released him. I didn't just forgive him for what he had done; I forgave him as a person loved by God, and I wanted him to know God personally. It was a life-changing moment for me. To this day, I have no idea where the chief is, or if he ever gave his life to God. Every effort I made to locate him was unsuccessful. When I think of the chief, there is no pain, only a hope and prayer that he discovered the love of Christ.

As soon as I released the chief, I felt the warmth of God's love. I knew that I had truly forgiven the man who had violated me. It would have been incredible if I could have forgiven him in person. He didn't need to be involved in the process because forgiveness can be one way; straight from my heart into his. When I had released all he had done against me, God filled that place inside me with a peace about the chief, and yes, even a love for him. I know that was God's grace because it was not natural; it was supernatural. This was one of my many miracles of God's *Grace Like Rain* over my life.

I haven't mentioned my dad much throughout these chapters. As I shared earlier, I always adored my father, yet felt displaced when he remarried and drew the line in the sand preventing us from mentioning our mom. I think he had assumed that when she and our three younger siblings were out of sight, they would also be out of mind. As you have read, nothing could have been further from the truth.

As God was pouring His *Grace Like Rain* over my hurts concerning my mom, He was also shining a light on the wounds left by my dad. His grace-infused forgiveness was not limited to my mom or the chief. God never limits forgiveness, nor should we. Forgiveness, much like grace, cannot be restricted; at least not by God. When God showed me that I also needed to forgive my father, it was easy because He had already graced me to forgive my mom, and the chief. When we forgive in one area, grace is set in motion to carry forgiveness wherever it is needed.

I have shared my story of forgiveness many times; it is my favorite chronicle of God's grace. Frequently people ask how I could have forgiven my mom, my dad, or the chief. It's a logical question, with no logical answer. I am God's daughter now, and as His child I don't operate from my natural mind any longer. He commands us to forgive, and as His daughter I choose to obey that command.

First Corinthians 2:16 says, *"We have the mind of Christ."* God has given us His Spirit and the ability to see things through His perspective, surpassing all logic. The bottom line for me is that God, through Christ, forgave me and saved me from an eternity in hell. If God could do that for me, how could I withhold the gift of forgiveness? Forgiveness is a gift. When you realize you have become a recipient of such a gift, it is impossible to withhold that gift from others.

God's grace enables us to forgive when we have been hurt and enables us to love when we have been betrayed. In the process, His distribution of *Grace Like Rain* over our lives enlarges our hearts to be even greater carriers of His gift. When God's forgiveness is grace-infused, it is more than an act or duty to be obediently adhered to by His children. It is a life force that takes us past the action of forgiveness to walk as forgivers.

The work of Christ's forgiveness through His death on the cross not only washed and cleansed us, but it permeated every part of our lives – past, present, and future – preparing us to be conduits of His forgiveness. This takes us beyond being a person who offers the gift of forgiveness, to *becoming a forgiver*. One restricts us to the act of forgiving; the other sends us forth as an ever-ready, grace-infused carrier of His love and reconciliation.

Being a forgiver means we are always in the game, never on the bench. When the need to forgive arises, we have already stepped up to the plate, and are positioned to be for others what Christ has called us to be: true forgivers. There is no need for the person to plead their case before us. We forgive because we have been forgiven.

As God began to renew my mind, my faith was fueled with understanding that God loved the chief just as much as He loved me. It may be hard to believe that about someone who once hurt us, but that doesn't change the fact that it is true. Grace levels the ground where we have piled up our reasoning, logic, and self-justification. Grace is God saying yes, even when we say no. Grace is God moving in one heart to release another from their offense. It was God's grace that gave me the willingness to let go. There is such freedom in forgiving.

Don't wait to forgive until you understand. That's where faith comes in. If our hearts are surrendered to Him, we can respond to God's call to forgive whether we feel like it or not. In forgiving the person, we are not only forgiving what they have done to us; we are also asking God to send His grace to wash over their suffering, their confusion, their history, and their humanity. When we hold on to what people have done to hurt us, we remain trapped in a dance of suffering with that person. In doing that, every time we think of them we remember what they've done against us. Instead, we can choose to blanket them with the covering of God's grace-infused forgiveness, which is all inclusive.

God used my experience in forgiving my mom to teach me that when grace moves in, it clears the room for amazing miracles of the heart. He equipped me with grace that extended into everything she had ever done, including her denial of my abuse. Once I opened the door of my wounded heart to His mighty rushing river of grace-infused forgiveness, it prepared the way for me to be a forgiver toward the chief.

God did the rest. He really did. He caused His own grace to move in and take up residence in my life, bringing with it a readiness to forgive the chief. Honestly, I had thought it would be next to impossible to forgive him for what he had done to me, but with God and His grace, all things are possible. He paid the ultimate price for our salvation; forgiving us and drawing us back into the relationship He always had in mind for us. How could we respond with anything less than hearts surrendered completely to Him?

Freedom comes when we choose to release the person completely. When we do this, we release them to be just like us – imperfect people desperately in need of God's grace. When we liberate others through forgiveness, we are also liberated. There are usually three parts to our forgiveness:

First: the Grace Gift. The *grace gift* is when, in obedience, we choose to extend forgiveness to our offender, whether they have asked for it, or are aware of their need for it. Neither matters. It is our responsibility and privilege to honor God by doing for others what He has done for us. We give what was given to us. God graced us. We get to grace others.

Second: the Grace Chase. The *grace chase* is God's movement of His grace into our painful situation, chasing down every area where we need His healing love and the true power of forgiveness. This stage can be instantaneous, or it can take time. For me, it took time with my mom but it was instant toward the chief and toward my dad. With my mom, I was at the feet of my Teacher, learning from God as He taught me not only the basics of biblical forgiveness, but also grace-chased my resistance and fear until I lowered the drawbridge and said yes. Saying yes to God's grace-chase opened the way for me to go past knowing about forgiveness, to becoming a forgiver. With the chief and my dad, all I know is when I extended the gift of forgiving grace toward each of them, I had a miraculous immediate healing in my heart toward both. I am still amazed at the power of God's forgiving grace.

Third: the Grace Place. We know we have reached the *grace place* when we think about the person and there is no more pain. We have extended forgiveness and we have released our offender. Even if the person who has hurt us does not understand God's grace, our cooperation with grace pushes their boat off its muddy shore and out into the extravagant possibilities of grace – positioning them to experience its beauty. This is my favorite part of grace.

When God infused me with grace to forgive my mom, He used the process to heal us both. As a result, my heart was made ready to extend forgiveness to the chief. Though I could still recall the acts of his abuse, my heart had been grace-washed and was no longer filled with hurt and anger toward him. I experienced the freedom contained within Christ-centered forgiveness. As God poured grace through me toward my dad, it was a father-daughter reunion of the hearts.

I have tried to imagine what it would have been like if I had been able to go to the chief in person and forgive him. Though it didn't work out that way, God caused a one-sided grace work in me; birthing a true prayerful desire for him to know the forgiveness of God and salvation through Jesus Christ. This was grace in action in my life. I learned to forgive without expecting anything in return. God overwhelmed me with His peace. *"And the peace of God, which surpasses all understanding, will guard your hearts and your minds in Christ Jesus"* (Philippians 4:7 ESV). Grace-infused forgiveness truly brings amazing peace.

Frequently in counseling, women have shared that hearing their abuser's name, or being reminded of the incidents that brought them pain, can resurface emotions they expected to disappear when they extended forgiveness. Then they would doubt whether they had truly forgiven their offender. When we forgive, I believe grace gets a green light to traffic in our collection of old feelings, but I do not believe that just because an emotion surfaces post-forgiveness it indicates that we never forgave in the first place. A heart that feels remorse when old feelings arise again has most likely forgiven, but still needs to continue in the process. Our experiences, feelings, and old mindsets about forgiveness must bow to the Truth of God's Word.

Grace Like Rain from His Word:

"But the Lord has become my fortress, and my God the rock in whom I take refuge" (Psalm 94:22).

"Then you will experience for yourselves the truth, and the truth will free you" (John 8:32 MSG).

"God means what He says. What He says goes. His powerful Word is sharp as a surgeon's scalpel, cutting through everything, whether doubt or defense, laying us open to listen and obey. Nothing and no one is impervious to God's Word.

We can't get away from it — no matter what" (Hebrews 4:12-13 MSG).

"Be kind and compassionate to one another, forgiving each other, just as in Christ God forgave you" (Ephesians 4:32).

"If you forgive anyone, I also forgive him. And what I have forgiven — if there was anything to forgive — I have forgiven in the sight of Christ for your sake, in order that Satan might not outwit us. For we are not unaware of his schemes" (2 Corinthians 2:10-11).

"Now we look inside, and what we see is that anyone united with the Messiah gets a fresh start, is created new. The old life is gone; a new life burgeons! Look at it! All this comes from the God who settled the relationship between us and Him, and then called us to settle our relationships with each other. God put the world square with Himself through the Messiah, giving the world a fresh start by offering forgiveness of sins. God has given us the task of telling everyone what He is doing. We're Christ's representatives. God uses us to persuade men and women to drop their differences and enter into God's work of making things right between them. We're speaking for Christ Himself now: Become friends with God; He's already a friend with you. How? You say. In Christ. God put the wrong on Him who never did anything wrong, so we could be put right with God" (2 Corinthians 5:17-21 MSG).

chapter twelve

GRACE FOR THE P-R-O-C-E-S-S

"Friends, when life gets really difficult,
don't jump to the conclusion
that God isn't on the job. Instead, be glad
that you are in the very thick
of what Christ experienced. This is a
spiritual refining process,
with glory just around the corner."
1 Peter 4:12-13 MSG

Every aspect of my journey in experiencing God's *Grace Like Rain* has involved process. Merriam-Webster defines process as *a natural phenomenon marked by gradual changes that lead toward a particular result; a series of actions or operations conducing to an end.* As we walk with the Lord, we discover that our maturity is developed through process. Over time, as we cooperate with what God is doing in our lives, His grace takes us toward His desired result. The problem with process is that we often get distracted along the way, and we get frustrated because we become more time-conscious than eternity-conscious. Remember, time serves eternity, but time is contained within eternity.

The *grace-infused forgiveness* that God worked into my relationship with my mother took several years. Yes, forgiveness happened in a split second, but the *process* that worked the fruit of forgiveness into our relationship, took much longer. By the time He awakened me to my need to extend forgiveness to the chief and my dad, my heart had been graced-over. I hope to give you a glimpse of some of the various ways God gave me *grace for the process*.

One of the most foundational aspects of *grace for process* that God wanted me to learn was the importance of learning to wait on Him. I confess; I have to return to this class often. When I am anxiously hoping for something to happen, I feel like a fidgety, distracted, interrupting grade-schooler. Psalm 37:7 says, *"Be still before the Lord and wait patiently for Him; do not fret"* (NIV). Fretting is not very becoming to a child of God. He tells us to wait patiently. For me, this means *don't argue; don't busy myself; just be still*. Sometimes we need to remove distractions so that we can be still and wait. It is good to wait on God. It is in the stillness that we are centered in Him, in His Word, in His peace, and even in ourselves.

By now you know that I am a believer in forgiveness. I love how I feel toward God when He moves me to forgive, and I love how I feel toward the one I choose to forgive. My experience in learning grace-infused forgiveness changed my life. I am a daughter of the Forgiver, and therefore forgiveness continually flows through my spiritual veins. God continually uses His *Grace Like Rain* to present me with countless opportunities to offer one of the best gifts of His grace: forgiveness. I guess it would be safe to say I am a *frequent flyer forgiver*. Each time we forgive a person, it sets something in motion in the spirit realm. We don't see it, we don't feel it, but over time that gift of forgiveness makes its way into another opportunity in another person's life for more grace.

I believe that forgiveness in its very makeup is exponential; it begins with a decision to forgive, our hearts are transformed, and then everything goes wildly out of control. Our eyes are opened and we begin to view the person as a son or daughter of a loving heavenly Father. *Grace Like Rain* takes over and spills and splashes out of control. Forgiveness then becomes a river within us, overflowing to others. If not interrupted by human reason, it becomes an unstoppable life-force that God uses to change us, change others, and ultimately change our world. Yes, *grace-infused forgiveness* is one of God's biggest exclamation points!

Six weeks before our baby was due, Mike finally agreed to attend church with me. I had been praying fervently that He would come to the Lord before the birth of our baby. The church service was overly crowded that night, and there was no place to sit but on the floor. Feeling a million months pregnant, the floor was the most comfortable place for me. I felt a little anxious for my husband when worship went exceptionally long, however, when I glanced at him to check on his annoyance level, he seemed curiously attentive.

As the service went on, the pastor preached an extended sermon, which also made me nervous. Annoyance check: again, Mike seemed fine. At the end of the message, the pastor gave an invitation to anyone who wanted to ask Jesus into their life, and have their sins forgiven. I felt my fingernails dig into Mike's knee, and at the same moment, I sensed the Lord was telling me to ease up. I guess I thought it was my job to make sure he got saved that night. As soon as I released my death grip from my husband's jeans, I felt his arm move. I opened my eyes, and that same reverse gravity that lifted my arm to the ceiling three years earlier, pulled his upward. My husband said yes to Jesus. This was beyond exciting!

We went to church every Sunday, and also attended midweek Bible studies. Mike was eager to learn everything about Jesus, the Bible, and how to walk as a believer. My husband had a unique conversion in that as soon as he said yes to Christ, he never uttered another blasphemous word. This was a big deal because he did have a foul mouth. (Sorry honey, but it's true.) His boss and coworkers immediately noticed his transformation, and this gave Mike an open door to share his new faith in Christ.

Six weeks after Mike gave his life to the Lord, contractions closed in on my baby's palace, and twenty-one hours later, Kevin Michael emerged. He was beautiful and passed his newborn examination with flying colors. As he was placed in my arms, I was struck by the calm and the ease with which we were suddenly a family. Mike and I were in love times three. Our introduction to parenthood couldn't have been smoother. I adored our new son, and loved being his mom.

When we sent out announcements celebrating Kevin's arrival, I set one aside for my mom. I added a Polaroid picture of our little family, wrote a note to her, and mailed it off. I was still learning the process of forgiveness. Little did I know that God would use my experience in forgiving my mom as the foundation for future opportunities to extend *grace-infused forgiveness*. I revisited God's classroom frequently to retake my forgiveness tests. Each time, however, I discovered that God doesn't grade on a curve; He grades on the Cross. No failure there; just countless opportunities to carry His forgiveness one more time.

When we forgive, sometimes we are impatient with the progress we see in the relationship. We don't know what God is doing in the heart of the other person. In my case, I didn't know what was going on in my mom's heart.

A few weeks after we had mailed Kevin's birth announcement to my mom, a package arrived in the mail from Colorado. It was a baby gift from my mother! I put Kevin on my lap and *together* we opened the package. There was a sweet card of congratulations and a nice note signed, *love, Nana*. I was ecstatic. God had indeed answered the desire of my heart. She had also sent a beautiful blue blanket and an adorable little blue newborn outfit. To this day I hold a vivid picture of that gift and card close to my heart.

Over the next few months, I corresponded with my mom, as she became increasingly attentive to my new roles as wife and mother. About six months after Kevin's birth, the phone rang, and when I heard my mom's voice I could hardly speak. I didn't know what to say. We stumbled awkwardly through a few opening lines, and then Kevin's cry seemed to break the ice. I picked him up and as she heard his sweet baby noises, our conversation unfolded as if we had never been apart. We chatted for over an hour, and then almost every month. We never talked about the past. It was as if we had made a silent pact not to go there. I was okay with that; after all, my mom was back in my life.

Mike and I spent a lot of time at church and with church friends. Mike's sisters had children close to the same time, so we enjoyed connecting and sharing our new season of motherhood together. We were blessed to have a few siblings on both sides of our families live nearby. Realizing that God had called us to love and lead our child was not only a great responsibility, but a great honor. We wanted to learn parenting God's way. We were grateful to be surrounded by other young Christian couples who wanted to do the same.

Mike and I now had new common ground; we both had surrendered our lives to the Lord, and wanted to grow closer to God. We had such a hunger for His Word and we spent long hours talking, praying, and studying the Bible together. Before long we began to sense that God was calling us to something even greater: what I like to call *the more of God.*

Kingdom maturity, though it depends on the Word of God foundationally, usually comes through real-life lessons, and those involve process. The pace often seems sluggish and snail-like, as it gradually unfolds the next spectacular thing God wants to do in our life. I have learned that our journey toward our next stop on our way to God's destiny for us is not marked with flashing neon lights, or even post-it notes indicating we are headed in the right direction. In fact, our path onward may not resemble anything we have imagined, causing us to wonder if we could have missed our yellow brick road completely. God uses our confusion as part of the process in leading us toward greater trust in Him.

When we study the lives of men and women of destiny in the Bible, we find that there was often a gap between God's call on their lives, and the fulfillment of that call. In between the call, and the fulfillment of the call, is this annoying little gap that we call process. If we get distracted by the future tense of God's call on our lives, we can get frustrated with His preparation process in the present. We may even become discouraged and be tempted to give up.

It is necessary for us to understand that *there is grace for the process.* God uses His *Grace Like Rain* to fit us to the calling, and to fit the calling to us. Too often we want to rush out and attach our hook to anything that resembles our perception of God's next assignment for us. I have learned that God uses the time between the call and the fulfillment of the call, to break us open, empty us of what is not of Him, and draw us closer to His heart. He isn't using the time to increase our gifts and abilities, but rather to teach us to depend on His.

Jesus was always doing this with His disciples. They would get all high and mighty and arrogant, and He would cut them down to size. This passage is a good example of *grace for the process*:

"And when He had sent the multitudes away, He went up on the mountain by Himself to pray. Now when evening came, He was alone there. But the boat was now in the middle of the sea, tossed by the waves, for the wind was contrary. Now in the fourth watch of the night Jesus went to them, walking on the sea. And when the disciples saw Him walking on the sea, they were troubled, saying, "It is a ghost!" And they cried out for fear. But immediately Jesus spoke to them, saying, "Be of good cheer! It is I; do not be afraid." And Peter answered Him and said, "Lord, if it is You, command me to come to You on the water." So He said, "Come." And when Peter had come down out of the boat, he walked on the water to go to Jesus. But when he saw that the wind was boisterous, he was afraid; and beginning to sink he cried out, saying, "Lord, save me!" And immediately Jesus stretched out His hand and caught him, and said to him, "O you of little faith, why did you doubt?" And when they got into the boat, the wind ceased" (Matthew 14:23-32 NKJV).

Grace broke through the storm with the *presence* of Jesus as He walked toward the disciples. As He got closer and closer to them, they saw Jesus walking *on top of* the very thing they feared was *taking them down.* I had never been in a forgiveness storm like the one with my mom. I had never needed Jesus the way I needed Him then. But He calmed me, saying, "Diana, I've got this." He was there in the midst of my entire forgiveness issue. His presence was enough for the disciples and His presence would be enough for me.

When Jesus started walking on the water toward His guys and said *"Fear not, It is I,"* that should have settled everything. He was telling them to take courage. He is saying the same thing to us. He wants us to take hold of courage in the middle of our storms. Not because of the storm, but because of who Jesus is in the storm.

Grace also broke into the storm with the *provision* of Jesus. When Peter saw Jesus walking on the water, he said, *"Lord, if it is You, command me to come to You on the water."* In essence, he was trusting that the Word of Jesus would be his provision. Jesus answered with one word: *"Come."* Peter stepped out of the familiar, into the unknown. Jesus called him to do what He was doing. In the calling came the provision. This truth was a key to my forgiveness breakthrough. God was calling me to deeper levels of forgiveness, and He was offering His grace as my provision.

Peter got out of the boat and walked on the water toward Jesus, and when Jesus called Him to come closer, Peter began to sink. Jesus was not being cruel when He said *"O you of little faith, why did you doubt?"* (Matthew 14:31). Jesus was identifying Peter's measure of faith. He wanted Peter to recognize his need to fill his faith-bucket with the faith of Jesus. Concealed within each lesson is the process through which we will learn that lesson.

Peter responded to the call of Jesus to come out on the water, but between the call, Peter's response, and the face-off with Jesus, we find Peter's lesson. The same is true for us. Hidden within the intervals that often frustrate us are close encounters of a God-kind. When we get distracted by our own need to get things right, we can miss our opportunity to draw close to the Lord and learn to trust Him at a greater level. These are places God gives grace for the process; grace to learn the lesson in front of us.

I love this story because it shows us that, like the disciples, we can walk close to the Lord and still fluctuate in our faith. Peter started out doing remarkably well, using his feet as paddle boards as he walked on the water toward the Master. For every step Peter took, I wonder if he tried to dodge the *what if* arrows of the enemy. *What if* you can't make it from the boat to Jesus? *What if* you get out in the middle of the lake and everyone starts laughing and you sink? *What if* you get too far from the boat, and not close enough to reach Jesus? *What if* you get between somewhere and over there and end up nowhere? I wonder if Peter got distracted by some *what ifs* and began to drop below the surface of the water.

What about you? Do you struggle with your own internal dispute when you are in your in-between time? *What if* your kids don't turn out right? *What if* your spouse leaves? *What if* you lose your job? I had struggled with *what ifs* concerning my mom. *What if* she refuses my mail? *What if* she hates me? *What if* she never responds to my letter? *What if* my kids never get to meet her? *What if* she gets mean and mad and I don't even *want* my kids to meet her? I want to encourage you not to give in to those opportunities to doubt God and His grace in your situation.

The enemy loves to interrupt the sermon God wants to preach through your life. He would've loved to have done that when Peter started to sink, but instead, Jesus used it as an object lesson for the disciples and also down through the centuries for us today. If we have doubts, God can integrate them into His sermon. If we have fears, God can overwrite them before the sermon is finished. One moment Peter was strolling on top of the sea, and the next he was in it up to his armpits.

Jesus uses everything we go through as teaching opportunities. Jesus taught through the issues of life. He used adversity, accidents and incidents. When He was silent, He was teaching. When He was praying, He was teaching. He is not just teaching when He shows up; He is also teaching when He doesn't seem to show up.

I learned, as did the disciples, that it is what we do when we are left alone that determines how well we have paid attention in class. The storms of life locate us. We discover what we are made of when we are in the midst of our storms. If we stay mindful of that, we will be able to focus more on the purpose of the storm than trying to find the fastest exit out of the storm.

The bottom line is: we go through storms. Storms are part of our process in going to the next level with the Lord. In Isaiah 43:1-2, God says, *"Don't be afraid, I've redeemed you. I've called your name. You're Mine. When you're in over your head, I'll be there with you. When you're in rough waters, you will not go down. When you're between a rock and a hard place, it won't be a dead end"* (MSG).

When fear impaired Peter's faith and brought him to the end of his own strength, he called out to the Lord. Jesus then took him, lifted him, and they walked back to the boat together. I have learned that God tailors the storms of my life to cause me to lean less on my own strength and more on His strength. I come to the end of me and find Him. Storms take us to a place of increased dependence on the Lord.

When the Lord began to teach me about becoming a forgiver, it felt like He untied my boat from the dock and pushed me out to sea. Much like the disciples, I found myself in a storm; however, my storm was not external, it was internal. The center of my storm was a squall of confusion. I had no grid for the kind of forgiveness God was asking of me. Forgiveness without an apology. Forgiveness with unanswered questions. Forgiveness with no turning back. Forgiveness that doesn't make sense. I felt isolated in the midst of consuming dark clouds.

Just because you go to church, doesn't mean you won't go through storms. Just because you have a relationship with Jesus, doesn't mean you won't feel as though you are being swallowed up by the waves of uncertainty. The disciples had walked with Jesus, talked with Jesus, and been taught by Jesus. Sometimes it can seem as if the Teacher has left the classroom, and we, His students, are left to ourselves. During my learning process, it seemed as though Jesus had not only left the classroom, but that He had left the building. Teacher. . . gone missing! Of course, He hadn't, but these times of aloneness serve His greater purpose: utter dependence on our Lord. These times are the perfect place for grace.

Hidden within those empty, solitary times, God revealed more and more of Himself to me. By speaking audibly to me? No. By letting me feel His nearness to me? No. He used His Word. My desperation drove me deeper into His Word. I needed Him, so I found Him in the pages where His voice was not muffled.

This was my breakthrough. Within God's call for me to forgive, was the provision for me to become a forgiver. Woven into the fabric of every crisis we face, is God's provision; not only provision to endure, but provision to break through to the other side. If you are in a crisis and you need faith, know that God's provision is there. If you are feeling weak and need strength, know that His strength is made perfect in your weakness. Your provision is contained in the very makeup of your process.

God used several specific passages of Scripture to give me a new perspective on the concept of *process* in our lives as His children.

- *"As they pass through the Valley of Baca, they make it a place of springs; the autumn rains also cover it with pools. They go from **strength to strength**, till each appears before God in Zion"* (Psalm 84:6-7, emphasis mine).
- *"For in it the righteousness of God is revealed from **faith to faith**"* (Romans 1:17 NAS, emphasis mine).
- *"Now the Lord is the Spirit, and where the Spirit of the Lord is, there is liberty. But we all, with unveiled face, beholding as in a mirror the glory of the Lord, are being transformed into the same image from **glory to glory**, just as from the Lord, the Spirit"* (2 Corinthians 3:17-18 NASU, emphasis mine).

I love knowing that God is determined that we grow to be all He has in mind for us. For me, He is persistent when it comes to moving my thinking from the natural realm to the spiritual realm. He wants to take us from:

- *strength to strength* (Psalm 84)
- *faith to faith* (Romans 1)
- *glory to glory* (2 Corinthians 3)

Do you see the little two-letter word between each pairing? Between strength *to* strength, faith *to* faith, and glory *to* glory, is process. We love the main words: *strength, faith, glory*. It's that tiny little in-between word: "to," that we tend to overlook.

I remember as a little girl, being enchanted by the trapeze artists at the circus. I loved to watch as the strong, young, athletic woman would be suspended in the air, grasping the hands of a very strong muscular young man, whose legs were hanging from a trapeze far above the ground in the circus tent. The young woman is confident that the man is strong enough to hold her, and that he won't let go. They begin to swing the trapeze, using the momentum of their bodies to go back and forth. Almost in unison, all eyes turn to the other side of the tent, where another young man is also suspended by his feet, swinging his trapeze.

Everyone sits on the edge of their seats as each trapeze begins to swing in sync with the other. On each side of the tent is a man swinging his trapeze back and forth. One of the men is holding on to the hands of the woman dangling below. Spectators hold their breath for my favorite part: at some point, the man will let go of the girl, and when she moves through the air toward the other side, it is her dearest hope that the guy on the other side is ready to grab her hands.

They glance at each other and with signals known only to them; they acknowledge that the time is right. Her hands are released, and she gracefully sails across the tent. For a brief moment, she is in the air. She is out of the hands of one man, but she is not yet in the hands of the other. The place in between is significant, for she cannot get from one position to the next without a period of transition. The same is true for us; *we cannot get from one place of strength to the next without our in-between time.*

As God's children, we feel secure in His hands; we know He is holding on to us because we gave our lives to Him. We go through a period of time believing that, with God, we can do anything. We read verses such as, *"No eye has seen, no ear has heard, no mind has conceived what God has prepared for those who love Him"* (1 Corinthians 2:9). We get all excited about the amazing things that God has for us. And we should. Then we ask Him to take us toward the next thing He has for us.

Then, the unthinkable happens. We find ourselves living in between one place of strength and the next;

one place of faith and the next; one realm of God's glory and the next. We find ourselves in the process, the place of preparation, but often we don't recognize it as such. We may not realize that God is preparing us for things He already has planned for us. He has our next amazing thing ready for us, so He invests His grace in our lives to prepare us. In other words: *God is getting us ready for what He already has ready for us.*

Our heavenly Father is maturing us as He schools us in the areas of strength, faith, and glory. There is often a period of time between learning about forgiveness and living in forgiveness. As God was teaching me to forgive, He was also pouring His grace over me. If He hadn't been so patient in teaching me about forgiveness through my relationship with my mom, I doubt I would have been able to forgive the chief so easily. It's important to remember that God sees the big picture. We are part of it, but we are not the whole picture.

When we start out learning to walk in new strength, faith, or glory; we get excited because we are getting experiential insight into new spiritual realms. We think we are going to soar onward and upward in our new-found truths. And then, a friend leaves; we lose a loved one; our finances take a turn for the worse, and we think these are obstacles to our growth. The exact opposite is true. What we consider as stumbling blocks are actually stepping stones designed to prepare us for what God has already prepared for us. He doesn't deposit a level of strength in our lives and then leave us there. He takes us from that level toward the next. In between those levels, He uses circumstances to create exactly what is needed to develop what is lacking in us. As much as we would like to hope that these times would be swift, often they seem painfully slow. We need to be careful not to get caught up in the timeline of our own process.

In my experience, God has used four main avenues in His graced-over process to teach me about His forgiveness. The first was His gift of forgiveness that washed my life clean through the sacrifice of Jesus. Second, He caused Scriptures concerning forgiveness to come alive for my own life. Third, He also used His Word to demonstrate countless examples of men and women to whom He extended forgiveness, and who learned to forgive. And fourth, He has used every experience of hurt, wound, rejection, betrayal, and abandonment in my life to teach me how to not only extend His grace-infused forgiveness, but ultimately *to become a forgiver.* It's important that we don't resent the very thing God wants to use to form us into the person He wants us to be.

When we make the decision to become a forgiver, God provides us with one opportunity after another to practice. He shines His light into our past experiences and illuminates areas where we are currently offended, angry, bitter, or hurt; enabling us to forgive with His grace. In essence, *we become forgivers because we have been forgiven, and then enabled by God's grace to do the same.*

People ask me how I could possibly forgive my mom and the chief. That's a logical question, and I *did* struggle with the logic of it all. When I focused on fairness and logic, I could justify many reasons not to forgive. I could be judge, jury and executioner in my mind; however, when I let myself go there, I didn't like how I felt. My mood changed, my outlook changed. Whenever I allowed myself to look through the lens of logic, I realized it was like putting up an umbrella to ignore God's *Grace Like Rain.* But God's grace cannot be ignored. Grace goes beyond logic. Love goes beyond reason. And forgiveness goes beyond human justice. Asking a forgiver how they could possibly forgive is like expecting rain not to be wet! *Being a forgiver is who God calls us to be, and forgiving is what we do.*

In our process, in our place of unknowing, we can feel unproductive and disconnected from people and things in the past, and emotionally unconnected to the present. Yet our seasons of process are really a time of reorientation. On one level we learn what God has placed before us. That causes us to hunger for more. As He draws us toward the more, He reorients us to hear His voice in an entirely new way. These are the lessons we can only learn by spending time in His presence and giving Him access to our lives.

Grace Like Rain from His Word:

"The works of His hands are faithful and just; all His precepts are trustworthy. They are steadfast forever and ever, done in faithfulness and uprightness" (Psalm 111:7-8).

"And we know that in all things God works for the good of those who love Him, who have been called according to His purpose" (Romans 8:28).

"Wait for the Lord; be strong and take heart and wait for the Lord" (Psalm 27:14).

"I wait expectantly for Your salvation; God, I do what You tell me. My soul guards and keeps all Your instructions — oh, how much I love them! I follow Your directions, abide by Your counsel; my life's an open book before You" (Psalm 119:166-168 MSG).

"I'm sticking with God. He's all I've got left" (Lamentations 3:24 MSG).

"Did you go through this whole painful learning process for nothing?" (Galatians 3:4 MSG).

"Commit your way to the Lord; trust in Him and He will do this: He will make your righteousness shine like the dawn, the justice of your cause like the noonday sun" (Psalm 37:5-6).

"Trust God from the bottom of your heart; don't try to figure out everything on your own. Listen for God's voice in everything you do, everywhere you go; He's the one who will keep you on track" (Proverbs 3:5-6 MSG).

chapter thirteen

THE GREAT GRACE AWAKENING

On a beautiful afternoon in the early spring of 1974, I was sitting in the middle of our living room floor with Kevin, now ten-months old, playing with his roly-poly *Weeble* family. He loved watching the colorful, weighted, egg-shapes bounce back to an upright position after his attempts to knock them down. I wanted a *Weeble* heart. I wanted a heart that always bounced back in spite of the weights of life. My thoughts and our giggles were interrupted by the worn-out ring of our doorbell. I opened the door, and to my astonishment, my mother was standing on my front steps! My sister had decided to surprise me, and *surprise* would be an understatement.

As I stood in the doorway, somewhere inside me I think I pushed the pause button. My stomach was in knots; I felt my heart beat faster, and I thought I was going to faint. My greatest hope and my greatest fear were standing only a screen door away from me. I had always hoped to see my mom. I had always feared what that would be like. Now I realized that deep down, I had been afraid to hope. Hope takes us on a carnival ride that we can't control. We get in, the attendant fastens down the bar over our lap, and the ride begins. I felt that way about hope; it was both exciting and daunting at the same time.

If my hopes were too high where my mom was concerned, was I locked into a place from which there was no escape? Did I want to be locked into hope? Even typing those questions seems ridiculous, but I was afraid to hope because I didn't want my hope to be crushed. There. I said it. *"Hope deferred makes the heart sick, but a longing fulfilled is a tree of life"* (Proverbs 13:12). I had been down this road before; I was familiar with the sick heart part. But I could not ignore the longing for relationship with my mom. Maybe this was God's way of fulfilling that longing.

As I felt myself settle into the present moment, I realized that my mom and my sister were still outside! I'm not sure how much time actually passed as I stood there with my mouth gaping open, trying to wrap my brain around what I was seeing. In real time, it was probably only moments before I flung the door open. In two small steps, my mom walked into my home and ultimately, back into my life.

At times like this, I wish I could tap a certain key and the exact words I am feeling would type themselves onto this page. I can only describe the next moments as grace-filled. When our blue eyes connected, they did so through tears that could not speak; tears that though wordless, spoke volumes. I still thank God to this day for that exact moment. It was a grace-washing, grace-redeeming, grace-receiving hug that came next. God did more in that one hug than a thousand letters could have done. Without a word, my mom and I had our reconnection.

Then, (and I smile as I write this), my mom reverted to her proper, gotta-get-out-of-this-awkward-moment self, stepped back, and twirled around toward Kevin. Now I was watching my *mom* pick up my *son;* a truly surreal moment. I paid attention to my own feelings; perhaps protectively, perhaps just curiously. Surprisingly, there was nothing but joy in watching them connect. It was a grace visit, a grace visit that brought a *grace awakening* to my life.

That day I was awakened to a slice of grace that I had never known. This unnoticed slice of grace was God's best, behind-the-scenes, love for me. Between the time God invited me to forgive my mother, and seeing her face-to-face, He had done a miracle in my heart. I knew I had forgiven her prior to her visit, but I had no idea how deep that grace-banked river went. In all the ways my mind had played out the scene of my reunion with my mother, I never expected that grace would cause it to be uncomplicated. I had envisioned awkward, rigid moments. I had expected discomfort, or even harsh word exchanges. But I had not expected this. I had not expected grace to make a way where there seemed to be no way. I was being awakened to a grace that goes the extra mile.

I know now that even though I was just wetting my toes in all that God had in store for me, I was in the river. Once you get in the river that flows with forgiving grace, you are positioned for miracles of the heart. I didn't know the extent of what God was doing in my heart toward my mom, but as I stood there looking into her sky blue, tear-filled eyes, I felt as if I was waking up to a new heart.

Only God could break me free from the childhood pain I felt concerning my mom. The grace awakening I experienced that day, in fixed eye-to-eye connection, erupted in a surge of love. I knew God had drenched me in His loving grace and presented me to my mother. God's love through us is effortless and liberating. It frees both the giver and receiver of forgiveness. Contained within the grace-washing river of forgiveness was an incredible release.

God showed me that I had been keeping my expectations low regarding restoration with my mom. If I hoped for little, maybe I wouldn't be disappointed. He wanted more. He wanted eternity-based hope. Eternity-based hope is future-centered. It sees beyond limits and hopes with purpose. Eternity-based hope contained my mother's ultimate need for an encounter with her heavenly Father. When God deposited this truth into my spirit, He also provided enabling grace to go the distance toward that purpose.

As we let go of anger, bitterness, and unforgiveness, we release our hearts to be carriers of His grace. This invites a move of His Spirit in our life as well as the life of the one we have forgiven. When I said yes to forgive my mom, I inadvertently said yes to a downpour of God's love toward us both; which graced the intersection of our two hearts. The wild, free-flowing current of God's grace unstopped every obstruction previously blocked by unforgiveness.

The Great Grace Awakening

That day, I was awakened to one of God's greatest gifts to my heart. When I gazed at my mom for those protracted moments, I recognized my mother's value in the sight of my Father. I recognized that He wanted to love her through me to reclaim her for His Kingdom. Grace can help us catch the vision of what someone can become, in spite of what they have been or done. Grace can cause a burning desire in our hearts to be a part of another person's transformation process. I knew at that moment that God had a greater purpose than just a mother-daughter reunion. He had a grace plan for my mom, and I was invited!

God's grace used this revelation to wash over places in my heart that I had thought were already healed, and took them through what would be likened to the soak-cycle in a washing machine. He was grace-soaking my *No Chair for Me* and my *Day I Lost My Voice* places. Now I was filled with excitement for my mom to come to know the Lord. I knew God had purposed a place of belonging for me in His plan. I also knew that He wanted to use my voice to love her to Christ. I call it an awakening because I think I had settled into a slumber of sorts in my heart toward my mom. I had become content with just knowing I had forgiven her. Now I was coming alive to the fruit of forgiveness.

True grace-infused forgiveness never settles. It takes us to a new level. I felt as if I was awakening without the usual sleep-induced crustiness in my eyes. I was now imagining my mom as a healed, restored, daughter of God. I knew that I wanted to have a part in God's plan for her, whatever that might be. *"No one's ever seen or heard anything like this, never so much as imagined anything quite like it — what God has arranged for those who love Him"* (1 Corinthians 2:9 MSG).

Over the next days of her brief visit, I had many opportunities to practice grace. I had assumed that since I had chosen to view my mom with God's grace and purpose over her life; rebuilding our relationship would be easy. Grace doesn't promise us that the road will be easy, it only promises to sustain us on the journey.

As we shared the remainder of our time together, I recognized my great need for enduring grace. What I had hoped for, as a result of my great awakening, was that God would allow me to be a refreshing pool of love and kindness to my mother on her path toward Christ. What I encountered, however, was incessant bumbling and stumbling over myself. I found myself misinterpreting statements made by my mom, which caused me to trek down old familiar bunny trails in my mind.

I hated some of the feelings that rose up in me when I heard references to the good ole days in Vermont. I needed to stand guard over my mind, like a sniper ready to take down lies whenever the enemy pushed rewind to play old tapes. I had to choose my words wisely so that I didn't slip back into my slimy pits of regret and shame. At the end of the day, I would sink into my pillow next to my husband, exhausted from doing battle in my mind.

Interestingly enough, at our church midweek Bible studies, we were studying the power of the Spirit-filled life. I knew God's timing was perfect. He used these teachings to deepen my awareness of the Holy Spirit's power to enlarge my heart and vision. In His desire to conform us into the image of Jesus, He uses situations that break down our dependency on self and increase our dependency on Him. Jesus was fully dependent on His Father, and He wants to develop that same dependency in each of us. The result will be a grace-endowed fullness that brings breakthrough in our lives as a result of Christ's finished work on the cross. I was learning to affirm my passion for Him to have His way in me. I truly wanted to be used by God in my mom's life.

There is enough sin, enough humanity in each of us, to put the squeeze on grace-infused forgiveness. As I mentioned earlier, the business of forgiveness can be done in an instant, but the place of forgiveness in our hearts must be frequently visited by grace. Simply put, when we are faced with an offense in an area where we have already applied forgiving grace, we may need to position ourselves for a fresh shower of God's *Grace Like Rain*.

I had to keep returning to the base of grace – Calvary. If I overrode my natural tendency to take offense, feel sorry for myself, or get angry, I could pick myself up and place myself at the foot of the cross again. When I did that, I could see my mom's need for God's saving grace through Jesus. This was amazing because I could see us on common ground. The common ground of grace is our need for Him. I loved the feeling of my heart softening when I could go there in my mind. When I felt my heart tenderize, I could feel the same love from God toward both of us. Equally loved. Equally valued. Equally died for. I could revisit this truth when I felt my heart ache in pain. I could go back to the foot of the cross and get my grace-fix, centering me so I could get back to the business of being a daughter: His daughter and hers.

God used the exhortation in Isaiah 52:1-2 to cause me to awaken to what He wanted to do in and through my life: *"Awake, awake, O Zion, clothe yourself with strength. Put on your garments of splendor, O Jerusalem, the holy city. The uncircumcised and defiled will not enter you again. Shake off your dust; rise up, sit enthroned, O Jerusalem. Free yourself from the chains on your neck, O captive Daughter of Zion."*

What is awakening? Broadly defined, it is a metaphor often used to describe any experience that opens us up to a previously unrecognized awareness of reality. My grace awakening, therefore, was God opening me up to a truth that I had not previously seen about myself, my mom, and God Himself. God was awakening me to take responsibility for my healing: to clothe myself with His strength; to shake off the effects of my history; to take the place He had given me in Christ, and to walk in freedom. He had made me aware of my need for freedom so many times before, but now, I felt new hope and new possibility. Now God would take me beyond my limited sphere of self, to extend His liberating grace to others; specifically, my mom.

This visit was proof to me of the transforming, healing power of God's *Grace Like Rain*. I had imagined a thousand times what it would be like if we were ever together again, yet I never thought it could go this well. Our time together during my mom's visit to Vermont marked the beginning of a new relationship. Her last words to me before she left were, "Next time, you and your family need to come to Colorado." I knew that one day we would take her up on that invitation.

Grace Like Rain from His Word:

"This is how much God loved the world: He gave His Son, His one and only Son. And this is why: so that no one need be destroyed; by believing in Him, anyone can have a whole and lasting life. God didn't go to all the trouble of sending His Son merely to point an accusing finger, telling the world how bad it was. He came to help, to put the world right again. Anyone who trusts in Him is acquitted; anyone who refuses to trust Him has long since been under the death sentence without knowing it. And why? Because of that person's failure to believe in the one-of-a-kind Son of God when introduced to Him" (John 3:16 MSG).

"From the fullness of His grace we have all received one blessing after another" (John 1:16).

"We know that we live in Him and He in us, because He has given us of His Spirit. And we have seen and testify that the Father has sent His Son to be the Savior of the world. If anyone acknowledges that Jesus is the Son of God, God lives in Him and He in God. And so we know and rely on the love God has for us" (1 John 4:13-16).

"There is no fear in love. But perfect love drives out fear, because fear has to do with punishment. The one who fears is not made perfect in love. We love because He first loved us. If anyone says, "I love God," yet hates his brother, he is a liar. For anyone who does not love his brother, whom he has seen, cannot love God, whom he has not seen. And He has given us this command: Whoever loves God must also love his brother" (1 John 4:18-21).

"I pray that out of His glorious riches He may strengthen you with power through His Spirit in your inner being, so that Christ may dwell in your hearts through faith. And I pray that you, being rooted and established in love, may have power, together with all the saints, to grasp how wide and long and high and deep is the love of Christ, and to know this love that surpasses knowledge — that you may be filled to the measure of all the fullness of God" (Ephesians 3:16-19).

chapter fourteen

GRACE CALLS

B efore Kevin's first birthday, the pastor of Bethel, the little house church we had been attending, announced that he and his family would be moving to California within the next month. This unsettling news was astonishing to our small church group of approximately forty people. In the short time we had been there, we had built relationships with many new friends. The pastor gave us a few suggestions to consider in looking for a new church home. After our last Sunday service at Bethel, we prayed for our pastor and his family, and sadly walked out of the building for the last time. This was a *grace call;* a call of grace that though unrecognized at the time, would lead us where we most likely would not have gone on our own.

Without question, every one of us knew we needed to find a new church home. Even though we were young believers, we had learned the value of gathering together to worship and grow in God's Word. One Sunday morning a few weeks after our pastor left, about three dozen Jesus People (that's what we were called), walked up the steps of Community Bible Church in South Burlington into our new home church; the church we have never left, and presently pastor. This church was different in structure, but not different in love, and we were welcomed with open arms. Two completely different cultures came together under the same A-frame roof and soon we became a blended family.

What we didn't know at the time was that the congregation in our little church had been crying out to God for a harvest. I'm not sure we were exactly what they had prayed for, but they embraced us, nonetheless. I think we were God's surprise package – all wrapped up in blue jeans – to this incredible group of people. We were undoubtedly a motley crew, in stark contrast to their more conservative, traditional attire. They accepted us without judgment or criticism, and exemplified *Grace Like Rain* over our immature lives. I am thankful, because beneath the jeans and t-shirt exterior, was hidden a fairly independent hippie mentality. I'm quite certain that if the church leadership had insisted that we submit to a dress code, we would have said sayonara and moved on to another church.

We planted our little family in our new church and began to grow through the teachings of our new pastors and teachers. We look back on our first months at CBC with grateful hearts for the patience and love of our church. Before long, we were recruited to teach Sunday morning classes for middle school kids. This would be one of many places I would hide behind my husband's gregarious confidence. He would teach, I would be his helper, and Kevin would join the toddlers' class. Studying and preparing to teach our class each week became an unanticipated occasion for us to grow in our walk with the Lord.

Over time, Mike was invited to run for the office of deacon in our church. He was hesitant, but our pastor advised him to let God speak through the vote. He followed the pastor's suggestion and was elected. This was totally out of my comfort zone because I preferred to stay in the background. God had other plans. As Mike and I began to build relationships in the church, several of the pastors and leaders and their wives took us under their wings. We are still friends with many of them to this day.

By this time, we had moved to a cute little three-bedroom ranch. Shortly after our move, to our elation, we discovered I was pregnant with our second child. At this point, our church seemed to be bursting at the seams with young families with babies and toddlers. We began a rotating weekly Bible study, which met at various homes. We prayed together, studied Scripture, and grew as friends. It was one of the places God softly and gently used His *Grace Like Rain* to help me feel accepted and valued. He was using this time to deepen my relationship with Him and with others.

As my mentors faithfully loved, encouraged, and believed in me, something profound was going on in my heart. There was a collision of all I was and all I was feeling pulled to become. Wounds from childhood were starting to fade into the background as my relationship with God was moving to the foreground. I was experiencing feelings like joy and peace. I felt a *grace call* to grow to be all that He had in His mind for me.

On Sunday, February 15, 1976, Mike's mom called to tell me she was coming to take Kevin home with her for the night. I bristled because I was still a few days from my delivery due date, and feeling a bit nervous about my toddler being away from me overnight. I loved Mike's mom. She was kind, giving and always made herself available to me. Unlike her usual cooperative nature, she insisted. I wasn't feeling any indication that labor had begun, but Mike thought we should comply. Kevin was excited to go home with his Grammy. Long story short, Grammy was right. Less than ten hours later, we welcomed a beautiful baby girl, Kimberly Lynn into our lives. We were in love with our family!

God had given me exactly what I had dreamed of; a son and a daughter. I was being awakened to God's love for me as *His daughter*. He wasn't a God who held back His best gifts. He wasn't a God who was waiting for me to do something perfect in order to get something I deserved from Him. Psalm 27:3 almost shouts: *"Don't you see that children are God's best gift?"* (MSG). I was overwhelmed by God's gifts of love in entrusting us with our two healthy, beautiful children. I had always wondered if God would allow a messed up, damaged, wounded person like me to be a mother. His demonstration of love in giving me the desires of my heart broke me open to know Him deeper.

There is so much I could share about my years as their mom, but it would be unfair not to provide a place here for them to tell you what it was like to have me for a mother. I am quite sure it wasn't easy for them. I was still working through my issues while trying to heal from childhood pain, and be their mom all at the same time. They had to try to walk the balance beam between the residual effects of my trauma and my joy in being their mother. They are both remarkable, loving adults who have far surpassed my greatest expectations as their mother. They have become strong Christ-followers; they have both made incredible choices for their spouses, and both couples are raising amazing children.

My mom and I continued our letters and phone calls, and it all seemed to be flowing quite well. Conversations were now filled with my reports of each new phase of Kevin and Kimberly's growth. Each time we talked, I was more thankful that God had brought us back together. Now that I was a mother, God was using my relationship with my own two children as the motivation to go the distance with my mom, no matter what.

When I told my dad that I had reconnected with my mom, he voiced his displeasure to me and told me how disappointed he was that I was rebuilding a relationship with my mom when his new wife wanted to have that relationship with me. I simply asked him to forgive me for disappointing him. I told him that was never my intention, but that now I was a grown woman, I wanted to know my mother, and I also wanted my children to know her. I told him I hoped that he would try to understand how much I wanted to be in relationship with my mom. God gave me a gift that day. I had already learned the power of asking forgiveness before extending forgiveness. We are humbled when we lay down our agenda for God's higher purposes.

Then God gave me understanding. I said, "Dad, I'm sure it was hard for you not to be close to your mom. I know that if you could have done something to change the situation, you would have tried." That was the turning point. Though it was rarely mentioned, I knew that my dad's mother had been hospitalized for mental instability. My dad's eyes welled up with tears, and he stammered out his acceptance of my apology.

Somehow God used the void in my dad's relationship with his mother, to bridge his heart to mine. He told me he was sorry that I lost all those years with my mother and asked for a fresh start. It was a grace-filled exchange. I told him how much I loved him and wanted him in my life. He received my words. I also said I wanted to be in a relationship with both my mother and my stepmother, and I believed that I could love them both. He thanked me, and when my dad hugged me, I felt God's arms around the two of us. It was as if we were both enveloped in His grace. From that point on, whenever my dad would call me, he would always say the same thing when I answered the phone: "How's my little girl?" I loved that.

My husband continued to work hard and put in long hours to make it possible for me to continue to be a stay-at-home mom. When asked how I learned to parent my kids after the debilitating trauma of abuse, I can only answer that God and my kids taught me how to parent. I couldn't say I wanted to be a mom like my own, nor could I say I wanted to be everything she wasn't. I didn't have that mindset. God used friends, other family members, and mostly my two children to teach me how to be a mom. I didn't always get it right, and I'm certain that my kids felt the effects of my history in my efforts to parent them. But I also know that God put a rather raw, unrefined predisposition within me to be a mom. Honestly, I think He puts it within every woman, though sometimes the events of life distort our ability to see our way through the debris of the past.

This was an unfolding role for me. As a little girl, I knew that I was born to be a mom. I wasn't sure of very many things, but of this I was absolutely sure. Though I didn't know the terminology back then, I knew as a little girl that my primary calling was to be a wife and mother. The word calling has slowly meant more to me, and all the more once I had children. It is one thing to want to be healed for the sake of healing. It is an entirely different thing to desire healing for the sake of God's greater purpose which is to portray His goodness through our lives.

I was becoming aware of the importance of reclaiming my voice; the voice I lost when I tried to tell my mom about the chief's abuse. *That voice.* God was showing me that my children needed a mom who was willing to go after what was hers; reclaiming not her past, but her future. He was awakening me to so many aspects of my life. Now I was a mom, and felt an urgency to have my heart restored. Each new day of motherhood brought with it an increased realization that my kids deserved a mom who was not still under the shadow of childhood shame.

God got my attention one sunny spring day when I had piled both kids in their little red Radio Flyer wagon, and strolled to our nearby park. Kimberly was just over a year old, and Kevin almost four. Each time I glanced back at my precious cargo, I saw the morning light glisten as it danced on their flaxen hair, causing a stunning halo-like effect. I loved these days. As soon as I pulled the wagon off the sidewalk onto the playground turf, there were simultaneous squeals of excitement at the sight of the swing set. Kimberly was happy to sit in the wagon and watch as I lifted her brother onto the swing. After a few pushes, Kevin fearlessly shrieked, "Higher, mommy, higher!" With each push, he wanted more. When I told him I couldn't push him any higher, he insisted, "Yes mommy, you can push me as high as I need. I need higher!" In that simple statement, it hit me. I had another *grace awakening.* God used a squealing toddler to teach me that in order for my kids to soar to the ultimate height God had for them, mommy needed to be able to take them *as high as they need.* I could choose to stay limited by my past, but it would not only affect me, it would also affect my children. I could choose to stay crippled by trauma and allow it to keep me down, and ultimately keep them down, or I could trust God to free me so I could become the mom my kids needed. He was awakening me; I mean *really* awakening me to the importance of my personal emotional freedom. He didn't want me to settle into my role as my kids' mother. He wanted me to settle into my role as His daughter, so I could become the mother that He had in mind for my children.

"God brought me up out of a horrible pit, out of the miry clay, and set my feet upon a rock, and established my steps" (Psalm 40:2 NKJV). God had preserved me through

my experience with the chief, and now He was setting my feet on the solid rock of His Word. If I can't stand for myself and the truth about my own life, how could I stand for my children? How could I stand for others? This was unsettling, yet settling all at the same time.

God continued to teach me the importance of discovering my identity as His daughter. It is vital that we settle some things in advance of the inevitable trials and tests of life so we won't slip back into behaving as if we weren't His children. He's there for us. He's the Rock, our solid foundation. That doesn't change. The issue is: will we awaken to His truth that says we can stand on that Rock? My identity as God's daughter needed to precede my role as a mom. If I reversed it, I would be trying to do motherhood in my own strength.

I am still learning that when *grace calls*, God equips us to answer the call. If *grace calls* us to go deeper in our relationship with the Lord, He is waiting to take us there. If *grace calls* us to forgive, provision has been made for the work of forgiveness in our hearts. Wherever *grace calls* us, God meets us.

Little did I know what was ahead for me as I prayed the prayers that came from deep within my heart. I was about to discover that what God purposes for us in our tomorrows, He implants the corresponding seeds in our today. He uses His *Grace Like Rain* to water those seeds, and surprises us as He takes us toward our destiny. It is out of the heart of the love of our heavenly Father, that *grace calls*.

When God's *grace calls*, we can be sure that His grace is sufficient and capable of meeting its own expectations. The highest call of grace is that we live with the realization that this earth is not our home, and our limited tenure here has eternal value. *Grace calls* us to cherish what God cherishes, and love what He loves. God always has eternity in mind; He lives there. He doesn't want us to live from time toward eternity; rather, He wants us to be so eternally centered that we live from eternity toward time. Practically speaking, this means as my heart is fixed on Christ, and as I am seated with Him in heavenly places, I can view my mom from that perspective. As I do, He can work in my mom's life through mine.

God was doing a really precious work in my heart regarding my relationship with my mom. I felt a growing compassion for her, prompting me to pray for her to be healed from the deep hurts in her own history. I began to pray that she would find her true identity in Christ. In short, He graced me with His mercy for her. I wanted my mom to have a radical invasion of God's love in her heart. I was experiencing God's mercy, and when we feel mercy, tenderness emanates from us because tenderness is a mercy reflex.

When we recognize the higher call of grace on our lives, God cultivates courage to protect the treasures He places in our hearts. Those treasures are souls. The treasures of God's heart become the treasures of our hearts. Grace is fearlessly wild, and takes us beyond limits. Although we typically choose the safe and familiar paths of life, grace has no problem leading us on a pilgrimage through our valleys of trials, tests, and turmoil. Grace takes us by the hand, knowing where we must go, and how to get us there. Grace knows that the journey itself is a preparation process to ready us for what He has in store.

The privileged call of grace on our lives is to see Christ formed in the lives of others. The apostle Paul travailed over this: *"My dear children, for whom I am again in the pains of childbirth until Christ is formed in you"* (Galatians 4:19). I want to have a heart that has its roots planted in eternity, not stuck in my history. I love viewing my life as a vessel to advance the Kingdom of God to accomplish

His plans and purposes. I believe that the *grace call* sharpens our spiritual eyes to see from eternity's perspective, enabling us to endure what we do not enjoy, and welcome what we would prefer to dismiss. God wants us to not only consider heaven as our future home, but also as the vantage point from which we gain greater clarity about our reason for existence.

Grace Like Rain from His Word:

"I sought the Lord, and He answered me; He delivered me from all my fears" (Psalm 34:4).

"Trust in the Lord and do good; dwell in the land and enjoy safe pasture. Delight yourself in the Lord and He will give you the desires of your heart" (Psalm 37:3-4).

"I waited patiently for the Lord; He turned to me and heard my cry. He lifted me out of the slimy pit, out of the mud and mire; He set my feet on a rock and gave me a firm place to stand" (Psalm 40: 1-2).

"They overcame by the blood of the Lamb and by the word of their testimony; they did not love their lives so much as to shrink from death" (Revelation 12:11).

"Let grace, mercy, and peace be with us in truth and love from God the Father and from Jesus Christ, Son of the Father" (2 John 3 MSG).

chapter fifteen

THE WIDE OPEN SPACES OF GOD'S GRACE

*"We throw open our doors to God and discover at the same moment that He has already thrown open His door to us. We find ourselves standing where we always hoped we might stand — out in **the wide open spaces of God's grace** and glory, standing tall and shouting our praise."*
Romans 5:2 MSG (emphasis mine)

From this point on, I invite you to buckle your seat belt and put your tray table in its upright position as we fast-forward through massive chunks of time, stopping only at the grace points on our designated route. I want to seal these chapters with the wax of God's purposeful grace.

During the young years of my children's lives, God was teaching me exactly what the verse above states, to *"throw open the doors of my heart to Him, and discover that He has already thrown His door open to me."* I could trust Him as He was applying grace to my wounds. I knew that I wanted everything He desired for me. He was strengthening my sense of security and identity as His daughter, which was impacting my relationship as my mother's daughter. I emphasize this because it laid the foundation for all my future years, important years, with my mom.

While God is working on our hearts, He is simultaneously working on the hearts of those involved in our future grace encounters. He continued to unravel the knots in the areas where my fear, shame, confusion, and control were still tangled up concerning my mom. He revealed my fear of being hurt again, confusion around old questions concerning the chief, and finally, control. I still wanted to manage the places my mom would be allowed to walk on the fragile corridors of my heart. The fact that I wanted to maintain control indicated that I still needed to allow God to dethrone my fears. The concept of throwing open the doors of my heart was next on His agenda in my grace walk.

During this time, our church held weekly Bible College classes and welcomed those who wanted to audit the courses. Mike and I were eager to grow in the Lord and took turns attending the classes, which were intense and challenging. The instructor began by discussing God's love; that it was relentless, intrusive, and forbearing. He used Ezekiel 11:19: *"I'll give you a new heart. I'll put a new spirit in you"* (MSG).

At the end of the class, the instructor gave an invitation to anyone who wanted to spend time at the altar with God. Grace moved me to the altar, grace accompanied me, and as I knelt down, I realized grace had also prepared me. God began to call me to a deeper place of surrender in Him. I knew exactly what He meant. I still had an arsenal of protection around my heart, ready to stand guard against anything that resembled an intrusion. I had this beautiful encounter with the Lord that night as

He offered me a new heart; one rooted safely in His. It was time to throw myself into the safety of His love. I was smitten by this overture of God's love and grace.

When I left church that night, I felt peaceful, and free. What I had not expected was the fountain of praise and worship that erupted from deep within my heart on my drive home. I had always liked singing to the Lord, but this was different. I believe He graced me with a new level of spontaneous worship that night. Prior to this encounter, most of my songs were my bellowing out my need for God to do something, rescue me, fix me, or heal me. Now it was as it should be, all about Him. I loved my new heart of worship. I loved my new heart, period.

On my drive home, I was transfixed with a new view of my mom. Up to that time, when I thought of her, I had been more focused on our relationship and my dreams for our future. Now I was praying that she would find freedom from burdens and that she would come to know the value her life has in the eyes of God. I had prayed similar prayers for her in the past, but usually with her relationship to me attached. This time it was all about her, and that excited me.

God's timing is perfect, and He was on the move in His desire to love my mom to life. In the fall of 1978, when Kevin was 5 and Kimberly was 2, Mike and I felt compelled to take our family to Colorado to see my mother and my three siblings. We had been praying for this trip ever since she had come to Vermont, and we felt the timing was right. We also knew this was more than just a cross-country field trip for us. When God orchestrates a Kingdom event, He does it big. God provided the finances, and my mom was excited that our family was traveling to Colorado, which she called "God's country."

We arrived in Denver on a stunningly beautiful afternoon. Mom met us at the airport and drove us through a most picturesque route to her home. On our first evening in Colorado, we were able to spend time with my three younger siblings, now all teenagers. I studied their features, looking for the little faces that I remembered. It was a surprisingly easy reconnection of our hearts. My mom and siblings loved meeting Kevin and Kimberly, who took to them immediately. After we checked in on our sleeping kids, Mike and I went to our room, and shared our excitement about how good it felt to be with my mom. We thanked God, and went to sleep.

The next day was packed with touristy adventures, including the Denver Zoo. Our kids had never been to a zoo, and their excitement filled the air. It was especially nice to step back and watch my siblings and my mom interact with the kids. After a long day, we settled back in at mom's condo, and she cooked one of the meals I remembered liking best as a kid: flank steak, garlic bread, and salad. Just tasting her food flashed back memories of the last time she had cooked it for our family. This moment was good, with no sadness attached.

That night is grace-marked as one of the best nights of my life. The kids were asleep, and Mike and I were now alone in the kitchen with my mom. She was leaning over the kitchen breakfast bar, and we were sitting on the stools. We were talking about our zoo adventure and catching up on family news, when my mom opened up an out-of-the-blue conversation about God and our relationship with Him. Her second husband had now passed, and she was seeking answers. She was seeking hope. Without realizing it at the time, she was seeking God.

Mike and I talked for hours about how we came to recognize our need for God, and our journey into His love and grace. We shared Scriptures with her, including the simplicity of salvation. She was reserved, but had a lot of questions. She asked the tough ones, like, "If God is so good, why does He allow bad things to happen to good people?" It was a sincere, emotional query. All we could do was point her to His faithfulness, goodness, kindness, mercy, and grace. We admitted that we didn't have all the answers, and assured her of His love.

I was calmly distracted by my own heart: *it was filled with love and compassion for my mother!* I was so glad God had been showing me that the larger picture, the one that wouldn't fit inside the frame of my issues; included this moment. My mom looked me square in the eyes and asked, "How can I know God?" Meltdown of all meltdowns. Three-way meltdown. Group hug. Mike and I shared John 3:16 with her and led her in the prayer that bridged her heart directly to the heart of her heavenly Father.

In my journey toward healing, I had come to know God's great love for my mom. I also knew that my heavenly Father was going to send His grace to chase her down, and most likely would use a human being to carry that grace. Call me selfish, but I didn't want anyone else to have the privilege of being God's ambassador of grace to my mom. It had to be me. I wanted God to do anything He needed to do to give me that privilege. I knew that God was pleased with my plea to be His grace-carrier to my mom's heart, and I wanted to cooperate with whatever He had to do in me to make that happen. God's *Grace Like Rain* had orchestrated one of the most beautiful encounters with His love that I have ever witnessed.

Friend, I don't know what you may have gone through in your life, but God does. I don't know what barriers may be between you and those who caused you hurt and pain, but God does. I don't know the condition of your heart, but God does. This is why I hold out to you my story of a little girl whose heart was crushed with pain, shame, abuse, and abandonment. This is why I hold out to you the heart of God that knew the condition of my heart, and used that pain to draw me to His heart. I share the journey of how God healed my heart so that you will allow Him to do the same for you. I invite you to see the bigger picture: that my need for Christ and my mom's need for Christ were no different. They were exactly the same. We were both sinners in need of God, and the only way to Him was through Jesus Christ.

Will you step into your calling as His child, and allow His grace to restore your life, so that you will also be able to extend that same restoring grace to others? I hope that you will. I encourage you to lay down any hesitation for the greater cause, and extend your hand to the one who needs to know their Dad, and then place their hand in His. Carry Isaiah 30:19 to that person and tell them they can, *"Cry for help and you'll find grace and more grace. The moment He hears, He'll answer"* (MSG).

When we throw the doors of our heart open to God, in our desire to be used in the life of another person, we discover that His *Grace Like Rain* has already been at work. Grace moves in ahead of us to welcome us when we get there. There I was, in Denver, Colorado, standing out in *"The wide open spaces of God's grace and glory, standing tall and shouting our praise"* (Romans 5:2 MSG, emphasis mine). God had given Mike and I the joy and privilege of introducing my mother to our Father. Now, just as my mom had indicated, it truly was God's country.

Grace Like Rain from His Word:

"For God so loved the world that He gave His one and only Son, that whoever believes in Him shall not perish but have eternal life" (John 3:16).

"So we're not giving up. How could we! Even though on the outside it often looks like things are falling apart on us, on

*the inside, where God is making new life, not a day goes by without His **unfolding grace**. These hard times are small potatoes compared to the coming good times, the lavish celebration prepared for us. There's far more here than meets the eye. The things we see now are here today, gone tomorrow. But the things we can't see now will last forever"* (2 Corinthians 4:16-18 MSG, emphasis mine).

chapter sixteen

GROW IN GRACE AND UNDERSTANDING

*"Grow in grace and understanding
of our Master and Savior, Jesus Christ."*
2 Peter 3:18 MSG

S ome of my most cherished memories with my mom were ways God allowed us to accompany her in her newfound relationship with Him. We mailed a Bible to her with highlighted passages that had helped us grow in our faith. We spoke regularly, and God faithfully helped us build our relationship. We contacted various churches in the Denver area and spoke with several pastors as we tried to help her find a church home. After visiting a few churches, she finally found one that felt like a good fit.

In each area where I had initially been reluctant in surrendering my hurts to the Lord, I became aware of His patience in teaching me to *grow in grace and understanding* of His ways. We don't always see His bigger picture, but as He takes us from one experience of His grace into the next, He brings increased understanding of the value of His great grace. I am eternally grateful for God's plan for my mom's salvation, and I am blessed that His plan included me.

The verse above taught me that I can choose to grow in grace and understanding of Christ and His ways. I prayed the prayer of the apostle Paul in Ephesians 1:18, asking God to *"enlighten the eyes of my understanding."* I didn't want to miss anything God was doing; not only in my mom, but also in my husband, my children, my own life, and anyone around me. I began asking God to break through my limitations so I could see His grace at work.

One example of God teaching me to *grow in grace and understanding* showed up in the classroom of learning to let go and hold on. I had put in my request for grace. I knew I couldn't walk down this path of parenting without His grace. I was beginning to recognize unfounded fears in releasing my children. God knew this and was faithful to provide ways to flush out my fears. The ladies of our church insisted I go on my very first women's retreat with them. I was resistant and reluctant. This was going to take me completely out of my comfort zone. I tried to rationalize my way out. *My kids are still too young for me to leave. They need me. There will be plenty of time for retreats when they are older.* Mike thought it was a great idea, and when someone anonymously paid my way, my last excuse was eliminated. So, off I went. Okay, I'll be honest: I hated every minute. I didn't like sharing a room with someone I hardly knew, and I didn't like being away from my kids. I was grateful for the kindness of the person who paid my way, but this was not for me.

When the retreat ended, I couldn't drive home fast enough. As I got closer to my house, I was flooded with guilt for leaving them at such a young age, and now worried that they might not be okay. *What if they had needed me and I wasn't there for them? What if they woke up at night crying for me?* As I passed the strip mall where the nearby movie theater was, I glanced at the marquis only to read the title of the movie currently playing. I couldn't believe my eyes. It read: *The Kids are Alright.* I'm not kidding! It was supposedly some 1979 documentary, but for me it was God using signage to remind me that He's got this. As you might imagine, God had targeted my maternal insecurities, and He hit the mark, dead center. We would be partnering in His desire to help me entrust my kids into His care. He was teaching me to *grow in grace and understanding* of His ways. His ways are always good.

Our little family seemed to be moving through the seasons of life at warp speed. Before we knew it, our son and daughter were moving through their elementary grades, attending class events, and church camps. These seasons forced me to learn to release my kids and trust them to God. Letting go didn't come easily to me. I wanted to protect my kids and thought that keeping them close was the only way to keep them safe. My learning to let go involved school, bus rides, new teachers, class trips, church camps, and anything else that was new and unfamiliar.

You probably have your own list of letting go times. For me, letting go meant that I had to step over old insecurities and fears. I wanted my kids to grow up as strong confident individuals, yet I didn't love the process. I was learning to use one hand to release them into God's care, while holding on to His promises with the other. This was much like strengthening a muscle. The more we use it, the stronger it becomes. Each time God taught me to walk in the grace to release my children, He strengthened me for the next time. I was learning to relinquish my need to protect my kids and trust my Father to be their Protector.

In the months and years to follow, God was not only working on my need to trust my kids into His care, but to trust Him as I stepped into the opportunities He presented to me. Before long, I was asked to substitute for our Sunday morning Adult Bible Study. I can remember one of our elders asked me to teach two Sundays in a row, and though he had given me a week's notice, I told him I needed a month's notice before I can teach. Why a month? Probably so I could calm my nerves and study the material a hundred times.

One Sunday night in 1981, we attended a church service that changed our lives. At the end of his message, the guest missionary extended an invitation to the altar for anyone who wanted to surrender their lives completely to the Lord. Mike and I both bolted to the altar. Neither of us knew why the other was going, but each of us wanted to do business with the Lord. When we got home that night we both knew we needed to tell each other what God had done in our private time at the altar. To our amazement, God had called each of us separately into ministry. We didn't know what it would look like or how it would come to pass; all we knew was that we had been called by the Lord.

We made an appointment to share this with the pastor and his wife, who admitted they weren't surprised at all. They told us they had recognized God's call on our lives and knew we would be pastors one day. They also offered to help us in any way possible as we prepared for ministry. Within the next two years, they mentored us toward our goal, encouraged our studies as we took the required courses, and celebrated with us when we received our ministerial credentials with the Assemblies of God.

Soon Mike was hired as the Assistant Pastor, and we trained in Pastoral Counseling. Our church opened up a Counseling Center; I began counseling women, and leading support groups for women who had been sexually abused as children. We taught Married Couples

Classes, led the Singles Ministry, and frequently taught the Adult Sunday School Class. I was asked to be the keynote speaker at an Adult Child of Alcoholics Seminar at a local Holiday Inn. God began to present me with countless opportunities to preach, teach, and share my testimony of His transforming grace.

Public speaking didn't come easily to me. Remember? This is the girl who cried her way through speeches in Dale Carnegie Classes. I wasn't skilled in communicating, but I had a heart to share what God had done in my life. I loved that God wanted to use me to pour out the message of His *Grace Like Rain* over my life, but the actual speaking, forced me to my knees. It was a place God wanted to dump grace over me, and I knew it. Each time I stepped in front of the microphone facing my audience, I also stepped into grace. My level of trust in God got amped up each time I preached. I could not depend on my ability or my self-confidence; I had to depend on God's grace to bring His anointing. That was my safe harbor.

I told God that I would be a willing vessel that He could pour through, but I also had a contingency clause. I told the Lord I didn't want to speak on a subject that I was not willing for Him to work into my life first. I knew that was a hefty clause, but I also knew I didn't want to *talk the talk* unless I was willing to *walk the walk.* Either way, I wanted to be authentic in delivering whatever He called me to deliver. God took me up on that, and most times, my learning curve for what I would share would be somewhere right up in my throat. I was usually pretty connected to my message; therefore, tears were imminent. Most often, the message He would have me share would be about the abuse by the chief, and my journey into God's *Grace Like Rain.* I knew that eventually I would be sharing about how God had healed my relationship with my mom.

When I told my mom what God was doing, I asked her for permission to share about our relationship and our journey toward restoration. I didn't want to violate the relationship that God had been restoring between us. Without hesitation, she tearfully agreed that if God could use our story, she would trust me in telling it. *She would trust me!* Her consent to let me share was a gift in itself, but for her to tell me she would trust me, was a grace gift to my heart. Now, my story could include my mom. After she released me to share, future messages often included my journey in learning grace-infused forgiveness in my relationship with my mom. No matter how hard it was for me to share my experience publicly, God was faithful in using my story to touch the lives of others. He opened new opportunities for me to speak across New England. Without exception, each time I shared, women came to me for prayer or counsel on how to begin their own journey toward forgiveness and restoration. God was bringing life and hope to others as a result of His *Grace Like Rain* in my life.

Over the next few years, Mike and I began to *grow in grace and understanding* about how to be in ministry together. Eventually, our pastor moved, and Mike was elected as the Senior Pastor. Our ministry journey is a whole separate chronicle of the goodness of God in allowing us to pastor such an amazing church. Our family went through all the typical adjustments that would accompany such a life change. Suffice it to say, we continue to pastor together at Community Bible Church, and we wouldn't want to be any place else. Our congregation is an amazing, God-loving, grace-giving family, and we love each of them.

We have been blessed in a unique way. Both my husband and I were raised, educated, married, saved, and raised our children within a five-mile radius of where we presently pastor. We have grown up with most of our congregation, which has brought the added blessing of having their kids grow up with ours. We have dedicated babies, performed the weddings of those same individuals, and then dedicated their children to the Lord. We are a generationally-minded church, and we share God's love for our community, our state, our nation, and the world.

Two months after Mike was elected as pastor, our church held an Installation Service to officially establish us in our new position. It was a beautiful event, with two services, and several ministers in attendance. At the end of the service, the minister gave an invitation for people to receive Christ as their personal Lord and Savior. The people weren't asked to come to the altar, but were given an opportunity to recite a prayer of salvation with the minister. God had an unexpected blessing for us in that service: my dad raised his hand and invited Christ into his life. God's *Grace Like Rain* had drawn my father into the love of his heavenly Father.

Growing in Grace and Understanding of my Dad

The spring after my dad gave his heart to the Lord, I led a book study at our church based on H. Norman Wright's book: *Always Daddy's Girl*. It's a wonderful in-depth look at a woman's relationship with her father, addressing issues that impact the father-daughter relationship. This study provided a great opportunity for me with my dad. There were sections in the book with guidelines for an adult daughter to interview her dad. My dad and I talked at length about the content of these interviews, including his childhood, his relationship with his parents, his school years, his marriage to my mother, and so much more. Without doubt, God was using this book to pour His *Grace Like Rain* over our relationship.

I believe God's grace gave me a window into my father's life, his heart, and his history. My dad openly shared with me what it was like to grow up in his home as a little boy and his journey into adulthood. With his permission, I was able to share what I was learning about my relationship with him in the study group. His candor in sharing gave the women hope to discover more about their own fathers.

Nine months after my dad gave his heart to the Lord, he drowned in a tragic boating accident. My grief was so raw and so weighty; I felt like I was sinking. I was thirty-eight years old; way too young for a daughter to lose her dad. I needed my grief to collide with grace. It did. It was a collision that spilled over into my dark reality and causing me to recognize God's sufficient grace. My experience with grief in the loss of my dad caused me to *grow in grace.* Grief wanders around aimlessly in our hearts. It bumps into responsibilities, crashes into routines, and makes simplicity complicated. If grace had not come to my side, I would have sunk into despair. God's *Grace Like Rain* goes with us into our grief, sustains us while we are there, keeps us from getting stuck, and enables us to move forward.

Second Peter 3:18 admonishes each of us to not only receive God's gift of grace, but to make a determined effort to *"grow in grace and understanding of our Master and Savior, Jesus Christ."* I love this passage. We are being called into greater intimacy in our relationship with Him. As I grow in intimacy with the Lord, I grow in my ability to trust His ways. I didn't feel prepared for my dad's untimely death, but God supplied grace for grief. In our last phone conversation, my dad said, "Do you know how proud I am of you?" That was a hug from my heavenly Father through my earthly dad. *Thank you, Dad... and dad.*

Grace Like Rain from His Word:

"That the God of our Lord Jesus Christ, the Father of glory, may give to you the spirit of wisdom and revelation in the knowledge of Him, the eyes of your understanding being enlightened; that you may know what is the hope of His calling, what are the riches of the glory of His inheritance in the saints, and what is the exceeding greatness of His power toward us who believe, according to the working of His mighty power which He worked in Christ when He raised Him from the dead and seated Him at His right hand in the heavenly places" (Ephesians 1:17-20 NKJV).

chapter seventeen

GRACE POURED OUT

"Grace mixed with faith and love
poured over me and into me.
And all because of Jesus."
1 Timothy 1:14 MSG

In 1994, God was pouring out His love and grace across our nation and the world. Churches everywhere were reporting lives changed, hearts healed, and passion ignited. Our church was one of countless places the Holy Spirit invaded with the revelation and experience of the Father's love. Every service carried a powerful anointing of the Father's love. We would stay for hours after a service, just to linger in the presence of God.

It wasn't that our church didn't know the love of God. We did, but not to this depth, and not on a church-wide level. This move of God was a shaking, an explosion; around us, upon us, and within us. It was corporate, and it was also personal. God's *Grace Like Rain* was flowing into our lives, displacing, and also replacing: displacing faulty mindsets about the Father's love, and replacing them with an experiential, healing sense of wonder. You know your heart is being awakened to His love when you would rather be in His presence than anyplace else.

We were experiencing God's *grace poured out.* Everywhere grace went, it carried a fresh deposit of the Father's love. Grace was poured out on angry hearts. Grace was poured out over troubled marriages. Grace was poured out over rebellious teenagers. Grace was poured out over lonely widows. Grace was poured out over broken relationships. Wherever God rained His grace, there was transformation: healed hearts, restored relationships, rekindled love, impassioned teenagers.

David said it well: *"God — You're my God! I can't get enough of You! I've worked up such hunger and thirst for God, traveling across dry and weary deserts. So here I am in the place of worship, eyes open, drinking in Your strength and glory. In Your generous love I am really living at last! My lips brim praises like fountains. I bless You every time I take a breath; my arms wave like banners of praise to You"* (Psalm 63:1-4 MSG).

I could write volumes about what God did through this time of bringing His people back to their first love. For me, this was God's *"grace mixed with faith and love poured over me and into me. And all because of Jesus"* (1 Timothy 1:14 MSG). I've shared how God used His *Grace Like Rain* in so many different ways in my life. Each one of those experiences had a part in changing me to bring me closer to Him and further away from the pain of my history. He had used those deposits to touch a myriad of places in my heart, but this was different.

Grace Poured Out – It's Personal

This great outpouring of God's love was more than a church renewal for me. It was personal. I had a growing dissatisfaction in my spirit. It wasn't directed at any person, or the result of anyone's behavior. I am certain that the dissatisfaction was God-sent. He does that. He takes us to a certain level of intimacy with Him, bringing growth in our lives as we mature in His Word. We could settle in right there, but God has a plan, and it's bigger than we can see at the time. Sometimes He allows a measure of dissatisfaction in our lives to take us to our next level.

In previous years, God would target a heart issue such as shame, effects of childhood abuse, fear, insecurity, and unforgiveness. Then He would pour His *Grace Like Rain* over that wound and bring healing. He would often bring healing through His Word, or extended quiet times which allowed Him to shine His Light over my soul. These are the times I experienced the deepest grace transformations. Even though each touch from God brought peace and fruit, I still had a deep longing for something more. I couldn't articulate it at the time; all I knew was that I felt like different parts of me were getting healed, but not my entire being. I would cry out to God and ask Him to show me what I might be missing so I could work on that area.

This outpouring was God's answer to my deepest prayer. It wasn't splashes of grace on random areas of my life. It was as if God picked me up and then submerged me into the depths of His raging river of love. A violent, wild river of grace. God's grace had introduced me to the consuming love of my Father. He was giving me a taste of what it really meant to be His beloved daughter. Now, God wasn't *fixing* my heart, He was displacing everything that didn't match what He had in mind for my heart.

Grace Poured Out – Rest

There was no striving in this place of the Father's love. I was beginning to discover God's rest. I had learned to be vigilant; standing guard over my own heart, remaining attentive to any possible intrusion. I had been so protective of my own heart that I was only giving God limited access to my heart. In that unconscious choice, I was keeping God's love at arm's length. I made a decision to surrender my arsenal of protection over to the Lord.

I found solace in the words of David: *"My soul finds rest in God alone; my salvation comes from Him. He alone is my rock and my salvation; He is my fortress, I will never be shaken"* (Psalm 62:1-2). This grace invasion plunged me into my heavenly Father's unconditional love for me. My heart had been longing for this rain of God's grace. Nothing remained dry. Every inch of my heart, my history, and my hopes were drenched with His love; not a concept of His love, but His actual love. I was experiencing His love; greater than I could have ever imagined and more powerful than I could contain.

In my personal spiritual renewal of the Father's love, each grace place was now under one massive deluge of the Father's love. It took me past what I had been learning about His love, it took me beyond my feelings of unworthiness about His love, and it blasted through every limited perception I had about the Father's love.

Grace Poured Out – A Voice Restored

I could not write a chapter on God's *Grace Poured Out* without including more about how He restored my voice. In Chapter Three I shared how I lost my voice as a result of my mom's disbelief. It felt as if the knife of shame cut my vocal cords. I want to bring this story full circle because it is one of God's best displays of His *Grace Like Rain* in my life.

The effects of my mom's disbelief when I tried to expose the chief's abuse were greater than I can possibly describe. It went to the core of my identity. My identity as my mom's daughter, yes. But even more seriously, it impaired my ability to receive the truth of my identity as God's daughter. We can't walk in our identity as children of God outside of intimacy with Him. Intimacy with God is the life source that fuels our ability to walk in our identity. I needed a breakthrough to be able to function as a daughter of God, and it had to happen in my heart.

I mentioned my secret longing to know my true identity in Chapter Seven. I needed to revisit the importance of identity to share just how vital this was in my restoration. If it sounds repetitive, it's because that is exactly my intent. If we don't take hold of the truth of our identity in Christ, we will forever be living from our natural identity, rather than what He has made possible for us.

As God poured His restoring grace over my shame and insecurity, He revived my deadened heart. I had learned so many ways to **do** life; I missed out on how to **be**. When I figured out what people expected of me, I learned all the right things to say and do. I shared earlier that I carried this over into my walk as a new believer. When I figured out what God expected of me, I learned all the right things to say and do where He was concerned. God isn't looking for behavior that is based on right and wrong. He is looking for behavior that comes from a heart that is right, a heart in right relationship with Him – *a relationship built on love.*

God did so much work in my life that isn't in these pages. He went to the core of my being and infused me with His love. It was love that saved me, and it was love that helped me discover my identity in Christ. When God showed me my eternal significance as His daughter, it melted me. It bypassed what my earthly parents did and didn't do for me. He used His Word to reveal Himself and myself. He taught me to trust that what He says about me trumps everything that has ever been said about me.

One of the most important truths that God revealed to me in my healing process was that even though my mom didn't believe me, He believes in me. This became a vital truth in restoring my voice. If you struggle with any aspect of your identity in Christ, invite God into your struggle. He desires to give you an unshakable identity. When He does, His *Grace Like Rain* equips us to say yes to anything He asks of us. I have come to learn that whenever God asks me to do something, it carries life. It carries the grace to obey.

I find it beyond incredible, beyond amazing, that God would ask someone who felt as though she had *lost her voice* as a little girl, to *use her voice* to proclaim the power of His transforming grace. *That's a really long sentence.* But it is one of my miracles of grace. As a result of His work in restoring me, it is one of my greatest joys to use my voice for Him. Each time He gives me the privilege of bragging about Him and His grace, I am reminded of His work in my life.

The platform from which I speak is not made of wood, carpet, or concrete. The platform from which I speak is made of raw amazement at the goodness and grace of a God who loves His girl. He did not call me to use my voice because I am a good speaker, or a master of the English language. Heaven knows better! He called me to use my voice because I am a daughter of the Master of the universe. I am loved and I will proclaim His goodness and grace until I have no breath. My voice may have been silenced by earth, but it was restored by heaven.

I encourage you to run past every obstacle and silence every echo that has tried to convince you that you have no voice. Your voice is rooted in your identity, and your identity is that of a child of God. *Speak!*

Grace Poured Out – Perspective Transformation

When God pours His *Grace Like Rain* over our lives, He brings a new perspective to our hearts. As you have read these chapters, your perspective of my childhood most likely does not include any good times or happy memories, right? That is precisely how I wanted you to view my life up until this chapter. I wanted you to understand that this is exactly how a person who has experienced childhood pain perceives her life. She looks at her life through the lens of her pain. If we do not allow God to rain His grace over our wounded places, we may very well view our entire history through the distortion of that pain.

However, as we surrender our hearts to the Lord, He not only heals and restores us; He also gives us the unexpected blessing of a new perspective on our history. The effects of my childhood trauma not only crippled my emotions, it paralyzed my perspective of my own life. Yes, I could remember brief interruptions to the sadness, but those seemed more like visits than truth. As God healed my heart, He also removed the layers of distortion, giving me a clear and healthy perspective.

I began to see that our family had been blessed in many ways. We had a gorgeous home on the lake, and my parents owned an island. We had a mobile home in Stowe, Vermont to accommodate our winter ski trips. God unveiled memories of boating, waterskiing, and my dad teaching me to snow ski by taking me down the mountain at age three; nestled safely between his knees, as I held on for dear life. I was now remembering that not every family dinner was tense, and not every interaction was laced with contempt. In fact, now I can smile when revisited by certain silly childhood memories, and then follow my urge to call a sibling and reminisce together. God resurfaced memories of huge family gatherings each Fourth of July, as we would launch fireworks from a raft on the lake behind our home. God accompanied me through dozens of happy memories with siblings, with cousins, with neighbors.

During future visits to see my mom in Colorado, we would pour through some of her photo albums of us as children, and she would describe activities and people in the pictures. Over the years, I have spent time with many of my siblings and they have helped me connect the dots, bringing back to life some happy times I had buried. When a person has endured childhood trauma, in her efforts to manage her memories, she often buries the good with the bad.

This is another vital aspect to our journey toward wholeness and healing in Christ. When He looks at us, He doesn't compartmentalize our hurts from our happy places. Remember, God has seen us from eternity past, and sees us in eternity future. In between, as we swing from one trapeze bar over to grab hold of the next, He wants us to be whole. It is my responsibility as God's child, to not only embrace His healing of my wounds, but also to embrace all the good memories that are part of my history.

Grace Poured Out – To Release and Rejoice

Over the next few years, Kevin and Kim graduated from high school and moved on to college. (I told you we would move quickly through big chunks of time.) Kim met Clint in high school, and Kevin and Maria met in college. Even though it was hard to release them into their futures, we were so grateful that they all loved God and were pursuing His call on their lives. If I could have selected life-mates for my son and daughter, I would have chosen Maria for Kevin, and Clint for Kim. God had answered our prayers in finding the perfect mates for our children.

In the year between Kevin's wedding and Kim's, my mom was diagnosed with terminal lung cancer. Several of my siblings and I were able to spend time with her as her condition worsened. In our moments alone together, my mom told me that she was quite certain she would not be alive to attend Kim's wedding. Even though I didn't want to believe it, we both knew it was true, and we cried together.

In true "mom" form, she pulled herself together and switched gears. She told me to go to the Dillard's department store where she had been employed, and I would find the mother-of-the-bride dress to wear to Kim's wedding. My mom was literally a *shop-til-you-drop* gal. She said, "Don't leave Colorado until you find your dress," insisting I get a blue one, her favorite color and mine. I couldn't believe she was on her death bed giving shopping instructions. I told her I would do my best.

During one of my last times alone with my mom, I thanked her for her life, and for giving me life. She told me how sorry she was for not believing my report of the chief's abuse. I told her I had forgiven her long ago and we cried together. She paused, put her hand on mine, and began to list reasons she needed my forgiveness. I interrupted her, put my fingers to her lips and told her that all was forgiven. I told her how blessed I was that God had restored our relationship, and that soon she would be pain free and with Jesus. I told her I would join her one day, and we would spend eternity together in heaven. My sister and I left the hospital that day, and soon after, my mother went into the presence of our Father. I was sad that death forced me to release her, but I rejoiced that God had done so many miracles in our relationship.

When Mike and I returned to Denver for my mom's funeral, I insisted that we go to Dillard's so I could purchase the mother-of-the-bride dress of her dreams. I envisioned God smiling over the irony: I didn't get the wedding dress of *my dreams*, and now I was getting the mother-of-the-bride dress of *my mother's dreams*. I had absolutely no doubt that I would walk into the store and find the dress.

We made our way to the store, and before the escalator reached the second floor, I found myself welling up with tears. *I really missed my mom.* We walked into the formalwear department, and I told Mike that God would show me the exact dress I was to take home. As I approached the rack, I flipped through two dresses, and when I got to the third dress, it was navy blue. I pulled it out, and knew I had found it. I tried it on, and of course, it was a perfect fit. I never looked further, nor did I ever try on another dress. It felt like a hug from the mom I had always dreamed would help me find my wedding dress. *This was even better.* This was God's *Grace Like Rain* over forty five years of life. He is an amazing Father.

Kim and Clint's wedding was only six months after my mom went home to be with the Lord. I definitely felt her absence. *Do you understand how good it feels to write that I felt my mom's absence?* This was more evidence of the miracle of *Grace Like Rain* poured over both of our hearts. I loved wearing my bought-by-insistence navy blue dress at my daughter's wedding.

My son and my daughter had now both married their best friends, and their new lives together as couples had begun. Now God was opening more opportunities for me to speak, not only in New England, but also Canada, New York, Florida, Nevada, and California. It was a little overwhelming if I focused on my natural ability. When I focused on God's grace to transform and restore my life, I was overwhelmed with praise for His faithfulness.

Grace Poured Out – Beyond My Wildest Dreams!

Within just a few years of the two most beautiful weddings ever, our kids began the next generation in our family. We were blessed beyond words as each baby arrived. Boy, boy, boy, boy, girl, girl, girl – seven grandchildren in as many years. I could expose my nana heart right here and go on a rant about each one of my grandchildren, but I'll spare you. God has certainly poured out His grace into each of their lives. At this writing, they range in ages from eight to fifteen; each one uniquely gifted and talented, and each one with a heart to serve God. I am blessed to watch them grow in the knowledge of the Lord and discover His plan for their lives.

Grace Poured Out – To Walk in It!

It's important for us to get God's perspective regarding our individual history. When we do, we see our lives in relationship to the bigger picture, His eternal picture. This helps us to understand what His *Grace Like Rain* has done for us, and also helps us continue to walk into our destiny, aware that we are a part of God's plan.

Regardless of what we go through in life, God has a plan. He uses His grace to disentangle us from our years of accumulated wounds and offenses. His grace enables us to freely offer forgiveness. As we allow God's *Grace Like Rain* to flow in and through our lives, we are set free, and we become a vessel for God to set others free. He uses us not only to carry His grace, but also to demonstrate His grace.

God's Kingdom is always advancing, always increasing, and we are a part of that Kingdom. As we continue to walk in an increasing revelation of His grace, we will walk with an expanded view, enlarged faith, and eager expectation of greater things for us, for our loved ones, and for our world.

Grace Like Rain from His Word:

"I consider everything a loss compared to the surpassing greatness of knowing Christ Jesus my Lord, for whose sake I have lost all things. I consider them rubbish, that I may gain Christ and be found in Him, not having a righteousness of my own that comes from the law, but that which is through faith in Christ — the righteousness that comes from God and is by faith. I want to know Christ and the power of His resurrection and the fellowship of sharing in His sufferings, becoming like Him in His death, and so, somehow, to attain to the resurrection from the dead. Not that I have already obtained all this, or have already been made perfect, but I press on to take hold of that for which Christ Jesus took hold of me" (Philippians 3:8-13).

"I pray also that the eyes of your heart may be enlightened in order that you may know the hope to which He has called you, the riches of His glorious inheritance in the saints" (Ephesians 1:18).

chapter eighteen

GRACE LIKE RAIN
FOR THE GENERATIONS

*"We will tell the next generation
the praiseworthy deeds of the Lord,
His power, and the wonders He has done."*
Psalm 78:4

A few years ago, I bought a beautiful thousand-piece puzzle of Noah's Ark to put together with my grandchildren. We laid out all the pieces, turned each one right-side up, found the edges and organized them into the frame. We puzzled (is that even a verb?) together for several weeks, a few hours at a time. Every time an area was completed, we celebrated, and then moved on to conquer yet another section of the puzzle. Excitement grew as we got down to the last few pieces. To our disappointment, when we put our one remaining piece into place, we discovered we were still missing one piece. We did a quick search of the table, the floor, and even emptied the vacuum cleaner. There was no getting around it; the elusive puzzle piece was nowhere to be found. The kids adjusted to our loss, yet still walked away from the table disappointed.

The next day I couldn't stop thinking about that one lost puzzle piece. We had spent hours working together around the table, and even discussed gluing and framing our masterpiece. The puzzle needed to be completed. I decided to go back to the store where I had purchased it to find a duplicate puzzle. I knew it was a long shot as it had been over three months since my first purchase. Regardless, I was determined and set out on my search. I walked into the store, headed for the puzzle aisle, and began rummaging around. At the end of the shelf, I moved one last box, and there it was. I felt like I had just won the lottery. I've never been more excited about Noah and his ark!

I bought the puzzle, took it home, opened it, and dumped the pieces out on my living room carpet. I separated out everything that was *not* bluish gray sky, and began my hunt for the missing piece. It wasn't long before I found it, and positioned it in its rightful place. I could hardly wait until the grandchildren's next visit. When they saw the puzzle displayed on my dining room table with no missing piece, they were elated. They asked where I had found the piece of sky, and took pleasure in hearing about my great puzzle adventure. They couldn't believe that I would go to such extremes to find just one little section of bluish gray cardboard.

They had that perplexed half-smile look on their faces. "Nana, you actually went to the store to buy another whole puzzle for just one piece! Why would you do that?" I loved that question. I let them know that our time together assembling the puzzle had been precious to me. I told them I had decided to do whatever I needed to do to find the missing piece. The responsive smiles and appreciation went far beyond the value of the twenty dollar box. They hadn't asked or even expected me to do that for them. I did it out of love and excitement to finish what we began.

God does that with us, doesn't He? He has the full picture in His mind where each of us is concerned and He has every intention of bringing that picture into focus for our lives. He does whatever is necessary to help us find our missing piece. He does more than we could ask or even imagine, and goes to any length for His children. I want to be driven by eternity; compelled to go the distance, no matter what it costs me.

I would have done my children and grandchildren a great injustice if I had not allowed God's *Grace Like Rain* to impact my life. Not only was it important for me to be restored for my own sake; it was vital for their sakes. When we allow the wounds of our history to define us today, we set a limit on our own potential. We need to tap into God's grace for complete healing so we can discover our true identity as His sons and daughters. Life is too short to stay paralyzed by our past. There are people in our lives waiting for authentic examples of God's love and grace.

If we want the generations that follow us to accomplish more than we do, we need to be a living display of God's grace. He calls each of us to become a container that He can pour His grace into, and a vessel through which He can release that grace. When we walk in God's grace we are releasing hope into the lives of others. Hope to dream for something greater.

You and I must believe that we can have a Kingdom impact for the generations. Throughout Scripture, God makes it evident that He is generationally-minded. Everything He has done in our lives is to be a megaphone over the lives of all who follow us. He wants to show others that what He has done for us, He can do for them.

We need to understand the currency of grace. It is never meant for us to experience and then put in an eternity account. It is meant to be given away. It is part of the legacy we pass on to future generations.

God went to the ultimate extreme in redeeming us. Jesus, in speaking of His Father said in John 3:16, *"For God so loved the world that He gave His one and only Son, that whoever believes in Him shall not perish but have eternal life."* There has never been a higher price paid in the history of the world. This utterly destroys any lies we have believed about our worth.

We must be of great value for God to send His only Son to take our sin upon Himself and pay the price that we should pay. He not only sent Jesus to die for our sins, but He raised Him from the dead victoriously so that we may rise victoriously out of any circumstance in life. God desires more than mere survival for each one of us. He desires a breakthrough beyond our greatest imaginations or dreams. He is already on the other side of our life drawing us to step into what He has prepared for us.

Have you ever seen an advertisement on television, and while you are watching, you get distracted by one aspect of the commercial, only to get to the end and wonder what product they were trying to sell? Your life and mine are advertisements for the goodness of God. He wants to showcase His love, faithfulness, kindness, power, and glory. As He displays His grace through our lives, others will be drawn to His saving grace and run to Him. Unlike those commercials, God wants it to be clear to the people watching our lives that He is a good God who loves them and has a plan for their lives.

When we allow God to touch our broken places, heal our hearts, bind up our wounds, and pour out His *Grace Like Rain* over our lives, He is glorified. He is honored. He is pleased. There is a generation behind us desperate to know that God has a destiny in store for them. They are yearning to make a difference in this world. They are watching the way our lives showcase the power of God. When they look at us, will they see lives healed, restored, and transformed? Will they see people whose lives have been graced-over, ready to do mighty exploits for the God we know and love? Will they see people whose hearts are rooted in another world, determined to make a difference in this one?

I share my journey, not because it is easy to tell, but because my heart has been flooded with a grace that speaks of destiny. A grace that shouts of purpose. A grace that carries hope. A grace that proclaims the goodness and faithfulness of our loving, caring, heavenly Father. Whatever your history holds in the darkness, allow Him to grace it into the Light. The Light of His love and Truth will dispel what should be dispelled. God wants to strengthen what He has placed within you, so you can carry your redemptive story to the generations. What God does in your life may be different from what He does in mine, but together, our lives paint a beautiful picture of His love and grace.

When God gives us a heart for the generations, it motivates us to make our life count. It motivates us to face off with painful issues that could hold us back. God has the generations in mind when He pours His grace over our history. As our children and grandchildren see God's transformation in our lives, they will be inspired to walk in a grace that brings even greater transformation. This is why the history of what God has done in our lives is so important. It is living proof to the next generation of His active involvement in our personal lives, and in our world.

Be of good courage, my friend; God has a multifaceted plan for your life. His *Grace Like Rain* is right on course;

first to re-establish your heart in wholeness and bring it back to life, and then to use the same grace that transformed you to touch every life He brings your way. You are part of an elite unit. You are a grace-carrier.

As sons and daughters of God, let us live our lives saturated with His grace, to impact a generation and inspire them to reach their potential for the King and His Kingdom. May each one of us leave a legacy of God's transforming grace. My prayer is that at the end of our days, it will be said of us as it was said of David: *"David had served God's purpose in his own generation"* (Acts 13:36). Let us serve God's purpose in our generation as we continually experience the downpour of God's *Grace Like Rain!*

Grace Like Rain from His Word:

"I will sing of the Lord's great love forever; with my mouth I will make Your faithfulness known through all generations. I will declare that Your love stands firm forever, that You established your faithfulness in heaven itself" (Psalm 89:1-2).

"Even when I am old and gray, do not forsake me, O God, till I declare Your power to the next generation, Your might to all who are to come" (Psalm 71:18).

"One generation will commend Your works to another; they will tell of Your mighty acts. They will speak of the glorious splendor of Your majesty, and I will meditate on Your wonderful works. They will tell of the power of Your awesome works, and I will proclaim Your great deeds. They will celebrate Your abundant goodness and joyfully sing of Your righteousness" (Psalm 145:4-7).

"But when He, the Spirit of truth, comes, He will guide you into all truth. He will not speak on His own; He will speak only what He hears, and He will tell you what is yet to come" (John 16:13).

"Now to Him who is able to do immeasurably more than all we ask or imagine, according to His power that is at work within us, to Him be glory in the church and in Christ Jesus throughout all generations, forever and ever!" (Ephesians 3:20-21).

CPSIA information can be obtained at www.ICGtesting.com
Printed in the USA
BVOW05s0546270314

348849BV00003B/12/P

9 781628 396331